Mom... You Just Need to Get Laid

Oct. 19, 2021

Susan,

Hope you enjoy all my NYC adventures! Always remember life is full of joy in possibilities. ♡

Kate

THE ADVENTURES OF DATING AFTER DIVORCE

KATE SOMERSET

Published in New York City by the Brooklyn Writers Press, an imprint of the Brooklyn Writers Co. LLC.

www.brooklynwriterspress.com

TITLE: Mom . . . You Just Need to Get Laid: The Adventures of Dating After Divorce

ISBN: 978-1-9529910-9-7 (e-book)
ISBN: 978-1-9529910-5-9 (paperback)

Library of Congress Catalog Card Number: 2020922372

1st Edition

To my beautiful daughter Ella,
whose resilience, straight talk, and courage
inspire me every day.

And to the movers who brought me to New York.

Without either, this book wouldn't have happened.

They both began to giggle and then they
fell into a side-splitting round of laughter,
the cleansing, complete sort of laughter
only a mother and daughter can share.

—KAREN KINGSBURY

Contents

Insider's Introduction 11

ANTHONY the Attorney 23

CUPIDO the Conductor 43

ANDERSON the Actor 61

MACK the Matchmaker 77

MARCUS the Manager 103

CAIN the Canine Lover 121

SAUL the Sailor 139

LEVI the Lawyer 157

EZRA the Entrepreneur 177

EARL the Engineer 191

STEFAN the Scholar 203

NICK the Neighbor 221

BRAEDEN the Banker 243

SAM the Solicitor 263

CHRISTOPHER the Connoisseur 276

Closing Reflections 295

Acknowledgments 301

About the Author 303

Thank You for Reading 304

Insider's Introduction

The Book Title Backstory

It was 12:30 AM on a summer Saturday night in Texas. The crowd in my kitchen was predictably noisy—my 18-year-old daughter Ella and her girlfriends had returned home.

After a night out, they were bringing the party inside. Carrying bags of In-N-Out burgers and fries, they landed in the kitchen, the command central in my house.

A hub of food preparation and consumption, the sprawling space was always where everyone wanted to be. The white floor, white tile backsplashes, white appliances, white cabinets, and tall, deep-set bay windows with their beveled glass panes were inviting. The views to a big lawn in the front and a red brick multilevel patio in the back situated the room for all-day and all-night activity, without missing out on anything that was happening outside.

And for me, the kitchen was also an office. My computer workstation, files, phone, notepads, and "to do" lists were neatly arranged on the non-food side, which gave a seamless transition from dining to doing. Except for dressing and sleeping, I hardly ever left the room when I was home.

That night Ella and Company commandeered the long kitchen island to consume their midnight snack. Regaling each other with jokes and stories from the evening, they used code words to keep me from fully understanding their meanings.

The giggles and snorts of laughter coming from Ella's crowd at the island were hard to ignore, even though I was across the room, absorbed in my latest email composition. Half of me was thrilled they were having so much fun. The other half of me was irritated by being disrupted when I needed to complete an important work project.

But all of me was glad that Ella was at our house with her friends. That meant I knew her whereabouts, not always a guarantee on weekends. It had been a challenging year for her and me.

After 24 years, I was going through a significant transition—a divorce that I had seen coming for years, a definite move from the house where I had lived my whole married life and raised Ella, and a likely shift in my career and work, a lot of those details unknown.

Several months before, my ex-husband had moved out. Even though Ella and I could now finally breathe different air, the removal of one other adult from the environment meant Ella's life just wasn't the same.

Having a mom working at all hours AND adding on all the responsibilities that come with divorce preparations gave Ella a lot of unsupervised freedom. And in her most vulnerable years. Even though she was an older teen, Ella's need for an active and present parent was still essential. I wasn't always physically there for observation and course correction. And so, she and her friends sometimes tested me, often in ways that made me laugh. Why didn't I see THAT one coming, I would wonder.

Ella's teenage friendships had been predictable in some ways and not in others. She moved easily in and out of her age-appropriate social groups, which included some friends who lived life in the fast lane. Ella could be a risk-taker. And she believed in speaking the truth and thinking about the fallout later.

At times more of an 'old soul' than a teenager, Ella often surprised me with her adult insights. And with a spot-on directness, she never minced words when tackling difficult or even verboten subjects.

It was Ella who first suggested the idea of divorce to my husband and me. Saying out loud the sentiments he and I had both felt but had never spoken, she boldly crossed a parent/child 'forbidden topic' line and never looked back.

Cornering us together over the previous Thanksgiving weekend, she had challenged us:

"You two are miserable. Why are you still together?"

That zinger of a question sparked the most honest conversation of at least a decade. And the upshot was that Ella had it exactly right. My quarter of a century marriage had run its course, and I needed to end it.

The three-way talk between Ella, my husband, and me happened almost a year before the In-N-Out burger feast in the kitchen.

By that night, divorce papers had been filed. And I was dealing with lawyers, accountants, and movers, while silently beginning to hatch a formulated plan for the new me.

And for the first time, I sensed Ella regarded me as a person, separating from my old life and taking control of my future.

Anxious to see who we both would be once the divorce was completed, Ella repeatedly asked why the process took so long. Since I had only an estimate of time, but no guaranteed end date, I could give her no satisfactory answer.

That frustrated her.

Toggling between complaining like a teenager or adopting a more adult perspective, Ella kept me off balance with her continued verbal poking and prodding.

This night was no different.

After she and her friends finished inhaling their burgers, Ella plopped into my desktop computer chair at the other end of the kitchen. I had gotten up for just a moment when she seized the opportunity, her friends circling her.

"Honey, you guys can't use the computer now," I said to her, as they began a Facebook search on a boy they had run across earlier that evening.

"Why not?"

"Because I have work to do, and besides, it's late, and time to bring an end to this party."

"Oh, Mom," Ella argued. "You are so controlling. Why are you so bossy and always telling me what to do?"

"Thirty more minutes before everyone has to go," I said to the group. "But take it to your room in the meantime," I directed Ella.

Her friends parted to either side of the computer chair. Ella slid out, rose to her feet, and looked straight at me with a funny little smile.

"I wish you could calm down and have some fun," she said.

And as she walked away with her friends in tow, Ella looked back over her shoulder at me. With an arch in her eyebrows, she announced matter-of-factly:

"Mom, You Just Need to Get Laid!"

Completely taken by surprise, I could only gasp:

"What?!"

"Yes, you heard me," Ella stood her ground. "You need a boyfriend. Then maybe you'd be human."

"You know that's not going to happen," I retorted. Her friends were laughing hard, trying not to look at me. "I'm separated and not divorced. And besides, if I had a boyfriend, your dad would have me with a millstone around my neck in a pond somewhere!"

"Are you EVER going to date?" she queried.

"I can't see it at all right now," I answered. "I don't think it's in the cards for me," I said honestly.

"Seriously, Mom, why?" Ella wouldn't let it go. "You should get out there and enjoy your life before you get too old. Honestly, you deserve to find someone who loves you. So, promise me you will date, AND that you won't forget about the OTHER thing I said. It will make you a new woman! In fact, I'm not leaving this kitchen until you tell me you agree."

By now, I was laughing. And I couldn't stop. And neither could Ella's friends. The more I laughed, the more Ella pressed.

"Mom, you just REALLY need to get laid!" she repeated, doing a little dance around the island.

To bring an end to the madness, and, in a moment of weakness, I offered her a compromise:

"Alright, honey. I'll make a deal with you. You're 18 now. By the time you're 21, I'll get that done!"

Ella came running towards me, poised to give me a high five. "I'm holding you to it!" Our hands slapped together. I couldn't believe what I had just agreed to.

In truth, I could not imagine any of it. I had endured breast cancer surgery, treatment, and the aftermath. I had been in a marriage where I was a housemate for fourteen years. I hadn't flirted with men, or even thought about dating, in almost thirty years. I was in the middle of a complicated divorce. Meeting men was not even on my radar.

My Epiphany

My divorce was almost finalized, and I was quietly contemplating leaving my old life and moving somewhere new. And then an odd thing happened. I noticed that men were engaging me. In a bookstore, a coffee shop, the airport, or even a gas station, I was getting looks, and conversations were starting to happen.

For 24 years of marriage, I had never encountered this. Under challenging circumstances, I was proud that I had been loyal, and the best spouse I knew how to be. Even though it was impossible to continue staying married, I was leaving, sure that I had given it my all.

I hadn't been looking at men, and they hadn't been looking at me. So, when it started occurring, I asked my therapist. "What could be different?"

"It's simple," he said. "The universe brings to you what you are open to receiving. You give off signals that let others know you are available. Availability can simply mean that you're willing to have a conversation. It can mean that you smile back. It can mean that you don't look away. It's subtle. And you may not even notice the shift in yourself. But it is happening. Remain open to the possibilities. And let your heart go there too. You have a lot of love to give. Enjoy the ride."

I left his office that day, thinking about what those possibilities might be. Six months later, I moved from Texas to New York. It was the hardest, scariest, riskiest, loneliest, and BEST decision I have ever made. In a nanosecond, my entire life changed.

Not only did I have new work, but I also had a new place to live, a completely different routine, and a fierce need to build a community for myself.

Why I Wrote This Book

At first, I resisted the idea of dating, especially going online to meet potential suitors. But within a couple of months of living in a completely new environment, it began to sound like fun.

I created an online dating profile. As with everything I do, I like to go big. And dating was going to be no exception. I joined five dating sites, and the journey began.

In two years, I have gone out with twice the number of men as the number of years I was married. Most I connected with online, but some I met in person.

Each date was unique, as was every man. As I accumulated stories, I told my girlfriends what was happening in my life. Their encouragement to share my dating adventures got me thinking.

How could I motivate others to step outside their fears? How could I demonstrate life should be taken less seriously? How could I be a role model for adventure and reinvention? How could I capture for others to enjoy, some of the craziest, as well as some of the best escapades that have ever happened to me?

I'll write them down, I decided. And the result is this book. I did it for me, yes, but also for you.

This book contains fifteen stories about fifteen men. I've chosen this group because they are alternately the most compelling, unique, or unusual of my experiences.

Names have been changed, but not descriptions or

circumstances. Each text and conversation are word-for-word (including egregious typos and poor grammar in one chapter in particular!) On occasion, I have slightly tailored events to compress timelines.

A number of these men continue to be good friends, (read my Closing Reflections on page 295) and they know their stories are included in this book. One said: "Please write anything you want about me! It will make me look so much better!"

Each chapter is a self-contained story.

Sometimes it's the tale of a single date. Sometimes the chapter describes a more extended connection. In every case, my goal is to accurately portray the men I have had the pleasure of meeting.

From funny to strange, from complicated to romantic, each date I have been on has made me stronger and more confident. I am grateful and appreciative that men of all different stripes and types have been interested in me.

And in every case, I remain interested in them and their lives. What have they lived through to make them who they are? What are their challenges, hopes, and dreams? How might I learn from their experiences, and they learn from mine?

From the first date to all the subsequent ones, I employ my style of connecting to better my dating experiences. I have always believed that we take responsibility for the quality of our relationships by the attitude we bring towards them. If we are genuinely thoughtful about how we interact, from not being afraid to initiate a conversation, to remembering details about another person, to authentically caring about them, our lives will be enriched.

I wrote this book to encourage you to view your circumstances in the bravest, boldest way you can. You'll discover MY version of brave and bold on these pages, including:

- Competing with a dog for a man's attention.
- Taking a friend as a chaperone on a date.
- Recovering after sending the wrong text message to the wrong man.
- Flying across the ocean to meet a man I had only known a week.
- Holding a man accountable for breaking an agreed upon plan.

We all face challenges in building and maintaining relationships. The best results happen when we put the best energy into them, consistently and with a genuine spirit.

Enjoy my experiences, and may you find joy in your own. Be open to the laughter, the surprises, and especially the possibilities. They are there if you look. I promise.

Who is Kate Somerset?

I wrote this book under a pen name. Kate Somerset IS me—in my move from Texas to New York, in my varied and unpredictable dating experiences, and in my belief in taking a risk and seizing the opportunities in life.

I lived thirty years of adulthood in Texas before hitting the New York City scene three years ago. I couldn't have written these stories if I hadn't made the move.

This book is born from my desire to encourage anyone who

thinks they can't or shouldn't put themselves out there. My writing under a pen name allows you, the reader, to believe that you can be Kate Somerset too.

We can all have a sense of adventure and curiosity. We can all enjoy life through the prism of friendship, kindness, and empathy. We can all see people for who they are, appreciating their amazing uniqueness. We can all have fun, in ways both big and small.

Believe that you can be Kate. She lives in all of us.

How to Read this Book

The fifteen men portrayed here are real people with real lives. My life intersected with theirs over a two-year period.

Chapters are not chronological, but read them in order to get the greatest enjoyment. You'll find clues to a timeline in a few. But you'll have to use your imagination to figure out the details. The illustrations and song titles are hints to what the chapters contain.

I hope you are amused, entertained, and touched. Share this book with friends who are dating, or thinking about it. The common experiences we all have help us know we are not alone.

A final note: This book was completed just as the pandemic began. The stories recounted here happened before our world changed. But I believe the universal desire for connection and finding meaning in relationships—no matter how or when we pursue them—will stand the test of time.

Mom...
You Just Need to
Get Laid

ANTHONY the Attorney

♪♪ I Gotta Feeling ♪♪

Artist: Black-Eyed Peas

It had been two-and-a-half months since I had moved to New York from Texas. Divorced almost a year, I had yet to convince myself that dating was important to me. But what I WAS sure of was that I wanted to make friends and meet people.

If going out with men was a pathway for making connections and building community, I was all in. Yes, I had heard the horror stories. But I had just survived an enormous move across the country. I could do this.

My life had already radically changed. It was time to keep my eyes open for all the possibilities.

And when it came to dating, I had heard and read that online dating was the fastest, and maybe the easiest way to meet people.

It was the last week in May. Eager to master the skill of meeting potential dates on the internet, I jumped in with both feet. Instead of choosing one dating app, I signed up for five: Coffee Meets Bagel, Our Time, Zoosk, E-Harmony, and Bumble. Each site had a unique process for enrolling. I spent late nights sitting cross-legged on my bed, completing all the application forms.

E-Harmony was the most comprehensive. Beyond the typical queries about hometown, occupation, work, age of children, and the qualities you seek in a match, applicants complete a lengthy survey. I gave thought to the essay-like questions, including:

- What are you passionate about?
- What do you enjoy doing with your leisure time?

- What are the three things you are thankful for?
- How happy are you?
- If your friends had to pick four words to describe you, what would they be?

I submitted my answers, which were compared with responses from potential match prospects. If the algorithms matched, I was shown a profile. Early the morning after E-Harmony officially accepted me, I opened up the app, eager to see what matches appeared.

The first profile I saw belonged to Anthony. A self-described rule follower, hard worker, Irish Catholic, Anthony had one adult son with whom he said he had a close relationship. He was thankful for a good education and the strict upbringing of his parents, both of whom were teachers (his father had originally studied to be a priest). Anthony had earned a full scholarship to college. He was a partner in a law firm where he had been for 37 years. He also had played with the same golf foursome for decades and described himself as a loyal friend.

I was thrilled. Anthony appeared solid, conscientious, stable, and driven. We exchanged messages back and forth during the day, and he proposed a phone call for that evening.

Wow, this is day one, and there are real people out there, I thought. *This dating experiment may be easier than I could have imagined.*

Our call began at 7:00 PM. When I answered the phone and heard Anthony's "hello," I immediately liked the sound of his voice: friendly, engaged, serious, and perhaps a bit flirty, but not practiced. I had no experience talking to potential dates on the phone, and no idea how a call like this should go.

What would he say? What would I say? What would he want to know?

Not waiting to find out, I began. “So, tell me about you and your life,” I said to Anthony. “You were born, and then what happened?”

Anthony laughed: “Are you a reporter?” he asked. But without any trace of irritation, he willingly answered, telling me about his family, his schools, friends, his two marriages, and his work in the legal profession.

“I grew up simply and having a lot of money wasn’t important. What matters most to me is education.” He talked at length and sounded excited to have a rapt audience. Four hours later, I looked at the clock and was shocked. Time had flown by. Anthony had told me a LOT about himself.

He had moved from downtown Philadelphia into the suburbs five years ago when he got divorced. “It feels less unusual being single living among lots of people,” he said. “I didn’t really want to get on the dating sites. I kept thinking I would meet someone, and it took a lot of energy to put myself out there. I am not really good at keeping up with people.

Besides my guy friends from college, from law school, and golf, I really don’t have a way to meet people. Everybody in my world is mostly married. I spend 80% of my time writing in the office. I bring the same salad every day for lunch. I am not a ball buster. Friends tell me that even though I am a lawyer, I am definitely laid back.

My sister pushed me until I finally agreed to go on the dating sites. My only rule when I first started was not to date women who had never been married or had no children. I didn’t believe that they could relate to me. And then my second rule eventually became only to date people who lived nearby. I didn’t think it would be worth the effort to travel to see someone. Frankly, your profile is so appealing, I was willing to take the chance. I would like to get to know you."

And so, we made a plan to meet.

"I'll meet you anywhere," Anthony said. Even though I lived two hours from him, Anthony offered to come to me.

"I can take Amtrak from Philly," he said. "My son lives in Brooklyn, so I am in New York all the time."

"Thank you for the offer," I said. "But I can make this even easier. In two weeks, I have an afternoon event just outside Philly. My train ticket is already purchased. Why don't I give you the homecourt advantage this time?"

"Great," he said before we hung up. "I'll figure out a plan for dinner and see you in two weeks."

Elated by the phone conversation and my very first date on the books, I sent Anthony a follow-up text:

"Thank you for the phone call. You told me you have met a lot of nice people, but there has been no chemistry. Well, I now have a new way for us to spell '*chemistry*'.

The "*C*" is for our four-hour (and one minute) *conversation*. It's your turn in the morning to tell me what the "*H*" stands for.

Knowing he would be asleep (Anthony had already told me he was a morning person and that 11:00 PM was his bedtime), I wondered how quickly he would answer me in the morning. Sure enough, the response came bright and early at 6:30 AM. I had been asleep for only five hours, but was wide awake when I saw his message:

"*H*" is for *her story/his story*—it's almost always interesting at this stage of our lives."

Not planning to answer quickly, I forced myself to wait until that evening. At 9 PM, I texted:

"I'll take *"E"* tomorrow. Get ready!"

Anthony pinged me back immediately: "Just as I was prepared to stay up for hours doing this . . ."

I started looking up words that defined 'chemistry' and began with *"E"*. There were plenty.

"I will be the first to admit that I am *eager* to give you this *entry*," I texted later. "I am *enlightened*, *entertained*, and *excited* to meet you! And I *embrace* the *effort* we are making for an *early encounter*. But since I made up the game, I am also making up new rules. From now on, let's go with one letter or one phrase. Apologies for getting carried away on *"E"*. My word is *electricity*."

The text from Anthony the next morning made me laugh.

"Whew. Glad to hear you say that, because I might struggle to come up with seven *"M"* words . . . I'll go with *mystery*, not in the sense of not knowing things about each other, but in the sense of why you find one person appealing, but not others."

Anthony continued enthusiastically: "I'll take *"I"* too for *interesting*. If you don't think the other person is interesting to talk to or be with, nothing is going to happen . . ."

"Ahh," I said. "You took two in a row. I forgot to consider that possibility when I made up the rules. You just want to see what I am going to do with the letter "S". You'll know tomorrow!"

Again, I waited a day before I sent Anthony the next message.

"I have been reflecting on the most descriptive "S" word. It's one of two phrases, but they aren't the same. Which one do you believe I chose?

Sexual attraction OR *sexual compatibility*?"

Anthony's comeback was clever:

"I was hoping you'd give me sex this morning :) . . . I think the second one."

This time, I didn't wait to reply:

"The first half of your response makes me laugh. The second half compels me to ask why you made that choice."

Even though Anthony was at his office by that time, he quickly came back with his answer:

"I think you either have a sexual attraction to someone or you don't, and that never changes (at least from my perspective). If you aren't sexually compatible though, that will cause a problem over time."

Our conversation on the topic of sex continued.

"Ah," I said. "I actually chose sexual attraction. Without it, you have no chemistry. And you usually know whether you do or you don't the first time you meet (no pressure!!)."

The day went by without another comment from Anthony. So, I was a little surprised to see an early evening message from him:

"Hi. Hope you had a good day. My client had other business to attend to. So, my colleague and I didn't have to take him out for dinner again. I was glad for the break and the earlier night. So, I can advance the game and answer you now. My "*T*" word is *trust*—you can't really enjoy being with someone unless you trust them."

Only two more letters to go to spell '*chemistry*'. One more from me, and the final letter from Anthony. Not to look overeager, I sent my last submission the next morning:

"*R*" is for *readiness*. A friend told me today that we often best connect with people when we aren't really looking. But I recognize we first must be willing to entertain the idea of meeting new people. In my case, I am finally at a place in my life where my eyes are at least open to future possibilities. Being in that place is part of our chemistry we show to the world."

I loved Anthony's answer:

"I'm glad I'm one of the possibilities you're open to!"

And I hoped he liked mine:

"I am glad that you are too! Now you have to bring it home with "*Y*". And by the way, I trust you. I feel very lucky you were my very first dating match!"

"Thank you," he said. "I obviously want you to feel comfortable with me . . . I think "*Y*" might be tough.

I was quick with a reply: "Unless you just go with '*yes*'.

"Just say yes!" Anthony liked it. "That's good, but I need to come up with something myself."

"OK, and I know it's past 10:30 PM and almost your bedtime. But I am not letting you off the hook," I challenged him. "Let's see what happens when you put that brilliant brain to work in the next 24 minutes."

Within seconds, Anthony sent his submission. "*Young at heart!*" he said.

"So perfect! Here is what we have," I recapped.

C— conversation
H— her story/his story
E— electricity
M— mystery
I — interesting
S — sexual attraction
T— trust
R— readiness
Y— young at heart

"Webster's would be proud!" I went on. "You think we got this?"

"Well, at least we have it down in theory!" Anthony hedged. "I am cautious by nature."

"Oh, have a little faith!" I countered.

"We have to have a little mystery when we meet," Anthony explained. "I'd rather find out more about you 'organically' on our date, so I'll reserve any opinions until then."

"Promises, promises!" I replied. "Wow, I kept you up past your bedtime several nights in a row. That could mean "TROUBLE!"

"I'm not complaining," I could almost hear Anthony smile through the phone.

As the time drew closer to our date, I contemplated logistics. I was going first to an afternoon outdoor work event in a city I didn't know. The required attire was casual. But Anthony was taking me to dinner at an upscale restaurant. Since I was traveling for two hours by train, I would need to freshen up, store my work materials and laptop, and change my look for the evening.

The only acceptable solution was to take a suitcase. But where would I put it?

I looked up the restaurant where Anthony had made dinner reservations and was happy to learn it was attached to the Philadelphia Rittenhouse Square, a five-star hotel. An idea popped into my head. I called the concierge at the hotel. "I am coming in from Manhattan for dinner on Saturday night," I said, "but I am headed back to New York City afterward. I am bringing a small suitcase with a change of clothes. Could I store my bag with the bellman?"

"Of course! Anything you need, Miss," came the answer. "We will be delighted to have you." John, the concierge, was now my new best friend.

The day of my meeting with Anthony finally arrived, and my anticipation ran high. By now, he had given me his last name, and I had read his bio on the law firm's website. His photo there was even more attractive than the one on his dating profile. A black-and-white image, the picture reminded me of a 1940s movie star, serious but approachable. I had also figured out a connection between Anthony's firm and one of my Philadelphia friends. Lucky me . . . my friend knew of the firm and of Anthony and gave an excellent review of both.

My level of comfort going into the date was great. All I could think was that this first date, with a man who was so easy to communicate with, might turn out to be really special. Was it this easy?

Up until the Saturday of our date, Anthony and I kept up the text communication.

"I dreamed about you last night," I said in one message. "We were to meet in the fourth car of the train . . . but then there was a power surge, and all the lights went out. I woke up, so I don't know what happened. You think we ever found each other?"

"I am confident that we did," he said.

"I guess there is a part two to the dream then," I surmised.

"You'll probably dream about something TOTALLY different tonight!" he retorted.

Saturday morning arrived. It would be a long day, but I was excited. Up at 6 AM, I got to Penn Station at 9 AM for my train ride to Philadelphia. I pulled a small overnighter and carried my work materials in a shoulder bag. Luckily, it was summer, so no coat was required.

Except for the Amtrak schedule change that almost made me late getting into Philadelphia, the rest of the day was picture perfect. The weather, the work event, and the Uber ride back to downtown Philly went off according to schedule.

I was to text Anthony when I arrived at the hotel from my event.

He would be waiting in the hotel bar. But I hoped to get there first, store my suitcase with John, and then make an entrance to meet him.

We planned to walk around downtown, get a drink, and then come back to change for dinner.

I had the Uber driver drop me off at the side entrance to the hotel. Luckily, that door led me right to the bell stand. And guess who was there? John! He immediately remembered me, greeted me warmly, and whisked my bag away. "Who could forget a Southern accent like yours?" he smiled. "Don't worry! Your bag will be right here when you need it."

I turned and realized I was standing in a hallway with a direct view of the bar. There he was.

In a navy blazer, button-down shirt, khaki pants, and reading glasses perched on the tip of his nose, Anthony looked as if he was engrossed in the transcription of a deposition.

I knew he was 6' 4", but I didn't have a concept of how tall that was until I saw him.

Earlier that day, I had sent a message:

"I hope that the 9" difference in our height doesn't require me to locate 9" heels! I have never stood beside a 6' 4" man. Does to be in your arms mean you have to pick me up? :)"

"Where there's a will, there's a way, but 5' 7" is not a problem :)"

"5' 7 ½"," I corrected him.

"That WILL be a problem," he teased.

I watched for a moment, unobserved. Then I called his name and walked towards him. Anthony rose to his feet to greet me. Towering over me, he hugged me. But it wasn't his height that felt awkward. It was his quick pullback. He seemed uncomfortable. Yes, he had smiled when he saw me, but almost in an instant, something had changed.

As we headed out onto the street, our strides were off. Each time I tried to match mine to his, I found myself bumping into him. After a few of those micro-collisions, I moved several feet away and then struggled to keep up with his long steps. Even if he wasn't exactly leaving me behind, he was certainly not making it easy for me to walk with him.

We crossed through a manicured downtown park and headed for an outdoor restaurant plaza where he suggested we have a drink. He stepped under an awning and took a seat at a table for two, which left me standing awkwardly by. It was a good thing I hadn't sat down, as a hostess arrived and immediately shooed us away.

"Those seats are reserved," she said. "You'll need to get in line at the front of the restaurant."

Looking a bit sheepish, Anthony strode ahead again until he found another prospective spot for us to light. This time, he made sure we could get seats at the bar. He took the first one for himself.

Our conversation over his beer and my prosecco felt forced. I marveled at the difference between the ease of our long phone call, multiple texts, and this. After what seemed like a very long time, he stood up, paid the bill, and suggested we head back to the hotel.

The return trip didn't go any more smoothly than our walk to forage for a drink. Relieved to return to the Rittenhouse and familiar territory, I told Anthony I would retrieve my suitcase and change clothes for dinner.

"Take your time," he said. "I'll go to the restaurant and wait for you there."

Switching from my jeans into a dress and heels, I pondered my situation. It was 7 PM and I had to make a 9:20 PM train. I had originally worried that Anthony and I would run out of time. Now I wondered if we could make it through dinner.

Satisfied that my dress, heels, and new jewelry were acceptable, I returned the suitcase to John. He gave a low whistle at my attire. "Go get 'em, tiger!" he said, encouragingly. "Your date is lucky to be with you tonight!"

The six-minute walk from the concierge stand to the restaurant took me past the bar, down a long corridor, and up a flight of stairs. I took my time, trying to imagine our dinner conversation.

When I got to the reception area of the restaurant, Anthony was not there. After ten minutes, I asked the hostess if he had appeared.

"Oh, yes, he is already seated at the table," she said. "Right this way."

Stepping into the dining room of the restaurant, I could see Anthony seated at a two-top, his back to me. He was staring out a huge plate-glass window onto a view of the downtown park where we had been earlier.

"Oh, hi," he said, looking up as if he had seen a ghost, and without getting up to seat me. "You look nice!"

The conversation at dinner was forced. I asked questions. Anthony answered. By the time the dessert menus had arrived, I was exhausted.

"We will have to hurry," he said. "I don't want you to be late for the train!"

"Let's skip dessert then," I responded. "I need to change back into my clothes for the train ride home. Thank you so much for dinner! I will meet you in the lobby in ten minutes." Anthony looked relieved.

I sprinted downstairs to get my suitcase and raced to the

deserted lady's room to change back into my afternoon work clothes. Locked in a toilet stall, I heard my cell phone buzz on the sink counter where I now realized I had accidentally left it. But halfway dressed, I couldn't open the door fast enough to retrieve the call, and the ring tone went to voicemail.

Rushing out of the stall to slap my things into the suitcase, I played the voicemail on my phone and was taken aback.

"Kate, it's Anthony," said a very out-of-breath voice. "What, what, what time is your train again?" he stammered. "I am trying to get the car and may not make it back. So, if you want to get in a taxi, go ahead."

I finished dressing and raced to the front of the hotel. Anthony called again. Still, out of breath, he said in a panicked voice: "Okay, be ready to jump in the car! I will be there in one minute."

Seconds later, Anthony's black Lexus sedan screeched under the porte-cochere of the hotel's driveway. He put the passenger's window down.

"Hurry get in! Throw your suitcase in the back," he yelled, activating the automatic lift for the trunk.

As I followed instructions and jumped in the car, Anthony pulled away from the curb with a jolt. He careened into traffic and drove a frantic ten minutes to the train station. With seconds to spare, he pulled up in front and told me to get out and run.

"But before you go," he said, "Here . . ." And with an awkward move, he leaned towards me and kissed me long and hard.

"Wow!" I exclaimed. "This should have happened a lot sooner."

Both shocked at the kiss and racing against the clock, I half-walked, half-ran, holding onto my heavy shoulder bag and pulling my suitcase into the station behind me. For a few nerve-wracking moments, I couldn't locate the gate for my train back to New York. When I finally got in line, I was the last person to board.

Once on the train, I had another two-and-a-half-hours back to my front door. I settled into my seat and tried to understand what had happened.

Was the Anthony I talked to on the phone the Anthony I met today?

How had the date been so different from what I expected?

Why had the build-up not matched the actual event?

"Made it!" I texted Anthony one minute before the train pulled out of the station. "Thank you! Loved this afternoon and tonight. (You weren't cautious at the end. Happy about that!)"

"I try not to be completely predictable :)" he said. "I had a great time with you too. I hope your day tomorrow goes well."

And with that, Anthony signed off. No text to make sure I got home. No text on Sunday. No text on Monday morning.

Finally, Monday at 9:30 PM, Anthony called and left me a voice mail:

"If you have a chance this evening, will you give me a call?" he said.

An hour later, when I got off the train and made it home, I called him.

"Thanks for meeting me on Saturday night," he began. "I enjoyed being with you. But in thinking about it, I want to let you know there is one thing I had not considered."

"Tell me," I replied. "What is it?"

"I am not down for a long-distance relationship. I just don't think this is going to work out," Anthony said.

"Well, I know you knew where I lived," I answered, pausing. "But I understand and am grateful I got to meet you."

After a few more exchanged pleasantries, we ended the call. For the rest of the evening, I thought about what Anthony had said. Something didn't add up. A day later, I sent him a message.

"Good morning, Anthony. Thanks so much for your call on Monday night. While I'm sad about the intent, I respect you for calling and telling me, and for being honest. Would you humor me to answer one more question since I am so new to dating? (Think of it as an exit interview!)

If we were in the same city, would you have pursued this? If not, why not? You can certainly say whatever you feel. I won't be offended. I am just trying to do the right thing the next time. So, if I was too flirty or pushed you too much or any of those things, it would be great to know.

I could tell you were disengaged. I just didn't know why. Thanks for even being willing to think about this. And if I don't hear from you, that will tell me what I need to know as well. Have a great day. Thanks again."

An hour later, Anthony answered:

"Kate, I'll definitely get back to you, but it might not be 'til later."

That evening, I got my answer:

"I'm happy to tell you what I feel," Anthony began in a long text.

"But keep in mind my reactions aren't universal. To the extent you date someone like me—somewhat relaxed, not a detail guy—maybe it can help.

Let me start by saying that I've never contacted anyone who lived so far away, but frankly I thought your profile was so appealing it was worth a shot. Given the complications involved in a long-distance relationship, I really didn't think it was likely we'd have a long-term relationship. I'm not used to so much communication before meeting someone, and we had so much, we already had a relationship of sorts before we met. I think this might have raised expectations a little.

As you probably figured, my preference is to know someone to some extent before meeting, and then to "experience" them when meeting, rather than finding out everything about them before meeting. For someone like me, that seems more natural and works better.

I think you and I are very compatible, and I could have talked to you for several more hours Saturday. One tip I'd offer is I sometimes felt like you spoke with me like you'd speak to someone you're dealing with professionally, instead of in a more relaxed personal manner. As a result, although we connected very well socially, I'm not sure how well we connected emotionally. Stated another way, I didn't get the feeling that you were "letting your hair down" with me.

Another tip I'd offer, related to something I said earlier, is to be more casual when first getting acquainted. In sports talk, it's called "letting the game come to you".

The bottom line is that I thought we were very compatible and good together socially, but probably not likely to form a strong emotional bond. I know this is kind of rambling and may say more about how I react to things than how you present yourself, but I hope it's helpful. You're obviously a special person, and I want all the best for you!"

Grateful Anthony took the time to write, but still mystified by his answer, I gave my best attempt to respond appropriately:

"Hi, Anthony, you won't be surprised that you are getting this from me way past your bedtime! I wanted to think about your answer. First, thank you. This was so helpful and honest, and I am grateful you took the time to write it.

Gosh, it's so interesting the conclusions we reach, what vibes we give off, how we communicate, and how first impressions are formed.

Your sharing yours really clarifies the experience for me. I'll take all of this to heart and I know learn a lot from it.

First, I understand how you came to the conclusions you did. And I think you are right about so much of this. Absolutely I did have my professional game face on. I have to admit that is an easy default for me. There is a whole other layer and girl to me. I am sorry you didn't get to meet her. Interestingly, she was scared to show up because I felt you were very formal with me.

Who knows? Isn't this confusion what causes countries to go to war?!

Anyway, I was concerned about doing something wrong. So, I did everything the way I knew how to do it. I need to think about behaving differently for dates with others.

Secondly, I know we communicated a lot before we ever saw each other. I was taking my cues from that four-hour phone call which was my very first . . . and by far the very best. I loved hearing your story and appreciated how much connection I felt to you then.

Third, I know you knew where I lived. Even given the distance between us, you had offered to meet me in Manhattan. So, I didn't think it was undoable to stay in touch.

I really do think we had a lot of similarities and I think you are a special person too. It was great to meet you. I wouldn't trade anything for it. I really hope all good things come your way, before 11 PM, that is. And here's my last rambling "off the record" postscript that might be helpful for you to know:

When you kissed me at the train station, everything changed. You went from being the guy I didn't know how to reach, to the one I wanted to get to know better.

So here is my one tip for you:

Begin all your dates that way, and you'll have 100% success! (My free of charge advice)."

"That advice shouldn't be too painful to implement," replied Anthony.

"Glad to be helpful," I answered.

And there ended my first lesson on why chemistry is everything in dating.

CUPIDO the Conductor

♫ Build Me Up Buttercup ♫

Artist: The Foundations

The greeting card was sandwiched inside a careening pile of newspapers, envelopes, memos, and magazines. The stack was placed on my work desk by my assistant, without much thought to the order of importance.

I had been traveling, and as always, there was too much to catch up on. Particularly challenged by the lack of organization, I absentmindedly flipped through the haphazard collection while returning the first of many phone calls.

Then I noticed it. Peeking out at an angle, the corner of a bright turquoise envelope caught my attention.

Pulling it out of the teetering stack of paper, I stared curiously at the handwriting on the front. All the words were hard to decipher—lettering that could be the work of a preschooler or a harried physician, featuring in equal measure careful pen strokes married to a messy childlike scrawl.

My forename was written grotesquely large with three letters "KAT" at least two times the size of the street address in the next line. The "E" of my name was tiny, trailing sideways down the right margin of the envelope. My last name, "SOMERSET," cascaded in an arc down and to the right, making me want to catch the letters before they fell off the side.

But even more than the scrawled inscription of my name, the sender's name in the top left corner ginned up confusion. It was a last name I didn't know, with an address I didn't recognize. The back of the envelope gave no clue. A Hallmark sticker sealed the flap. Hmmm . . . why was I receiving personal mail at my workplace?

I could contain my curiosity no more. I tore through the gold seal, opened the envelope, and pulled out a greeting card. On the front was a drawing of a giant chocolate bar. Suspended over the image of the candy were the words: "All I ever needed in life was chocolate". One corner of the bar was bitten away.

The inside greeting of the card read:

"Until I met you." And in a cursive hand, entirely different from the printing on the envelope, was a message scribbled:

"You're the first person who's made me feel this way. I can't wait to see you again. Cupido."

Simultaneously stunned at such a declaration of affection and at realizing who the sender was, I made a quick inventory of the events which led to my receiving this unexpected piece of mail.

The sender was a man I had matched with online. Initially, I had ignored his profile on the dating site, swiping left each time I encountered it. But then several days later, it would appear again.

The photo was appealing enough. A slight, well-groomed man of what appeared to be Italian descent, his picture featured him standing between two teenage girls. Both brunettes with pleasant smiles, each of them seemed happy to be there. Dad was both friendly and doting, and apparently eager to take part in this family montage.

My only concern was his name. Cupido. Very Italian. Very appropriate for a Valentine's greeting card. What was his mother thinking?

Since moving from Texas to New York, I had just begun to get used to all the Italian names. Vito. Gino. Francesco. Giovanni. Luigi. But this was a new one for me.

At least Cupido's clean-cut look didn't at all scream Casanova. And the description of his work was admittedly an intriguing hook:

"Don't hate me for what I do."

Besides being an IRS agent, what profession could he possibly have that would be that mysteriously unappealing, I wondered. I had to know. So, I sent him a message:

"Hi, Cupido, your profile keeps appearing in my inbox. That must mean either we are destined to meet, or my phone has a glitch."

He responded in seconds.

"Wow, I am so glad you answered me. I am sorry to keep sending you messages. But I can't stop looking at your photos. You don't look like anyone from around here. I would like to meet you. May I call?"

Our phone visit provided the answer to why Cupido's work might be unpopular. He was a train conductor. For the Long Island Railroad. Along with thousands of others, I rode those packed trains into Penn Station, in the heart of Manhattan. I had gotten used to the idea that trains and train stations, along with the conductors on board, were a constant feature of my new life.

So why did Cupido feel the need to cryptically warn prospective dates? Because travel delays, track maintenance and repairs, summer heat, and winter discomfort meant New York riders were quick to blame anyone wearing the train uniform.

But as a recent transplant from Texas, I found commuting by train both new and exciting. So, after hearing about Cupido's work, I was all in to meet him.

"Our lives are VERY different," I texted, "but I am fascinated by trains and would love to learn more."

To which he responded: "Whenever you are ready. Maybe one day we could meet in the City, and I could give you a tour of PSCC (Penn Station Central Control). It's very interesting."

I was quick to reply: "I really would enjoy that. My fascination with trains started when I was a little girl. There was a train track not far from our house when I was growing up. My sister and I used to put coins on the track so the trains would flatten them. And I loved drifting off to sleep at night, to the sound of a train whistling in the distance. It would be such fun to learn all about what you do."

"OK, but not over a text," Cupido said. "Hopefully in person, and you can tell me about you as well."

And so, it began. Knowing I was interested in trains, every few days, Cupido sent me photos of train tracks, train yards, views from train windows of sunrises, sunsets, and New York bodies of water I had never seen. It was my personal curated "ride the rails" travelogue by a real train engineer.

"If you like trains," he'd say,"you might enjoy these. Drawbridge and Long Beach yard!!" Or "Just a few shots from the Long Beach trestle!!!" One, two, or three train emojis would follow each text and accompanying photos.

Several weeks passed, and the messages continued, always with an invitation to get together. In each of the exchanges, Cupido would comment favorably on my dating profile photos and offer more information about himself.

"I could tell you I am 6' 3", 215 pounds and built like an Olympic bodybuilder, but I won't. I'm 5' 10" and 160 pounds. I was heavier about 4 years ago and not happy with my appearance, so I changed my eating habits and lost about 25 pounds and feel much better and am a lot happier with my appearance. How tall are you????"

Curious if Cupido shared his height in order to screen for women who wouldn't be taller, I may have eased his fears by responding:

"Good for you! I am 5' 7ish" and weigh about 127 pounds, except after eating apple pie, which is my favorite."

"Sounds nice," he responded. "You must be in good shape. If we keep talking like this what will we talk about when we meet???? Malverne pastry shop makes a great apple pie. And I cook a mean veal parmigiana. Maybe you could come over and I could cook for you. I like red wine. Do you like red wine????"

Cupido's giddy punctuation suggested *everything* was exciting.

I had the feeling Cupido would have told me whatever he thought I wanted to hear in those first few weeks. So eager to please, his innocent text messages had the feel of high school dance flirtations, where boys would search desperately for something to say and then exhaust the topic in the first sentence.

Both out of curiosity and amusement, I agreed to meet Cupido one Friday night. Earlier that morning, he had texted me he was free.

"Guess what?????" he began. "I had a shift change today. That means I get off at 9 PM and that also means I could take you for that glass of red wine you like. Please say you'll meet me. I promise you a good time. It's just the start of something great!!!!"

He proposed the date in an Italian neighborhood near the train tracks, on a street lined with small trattorias, bars, and butcher shops that looked as though they belonged on a mafia movie set. Building addresses were a combination of a number and a letter. Some of them weren't marked at all. And at 10 PM, I wasn't sure this would be a neighborhood I would frequent alone.

Reading the address was only half the battle. Finding parking was the biggest challenge. Cars were jammed together so tightly along the narrow street, it looked like a crane would have to extricate them. I circled the block three times, trying to stay calm about the neighborhood and finding a safe spot for my car.

Just as I was about to give up, Cupido texted me.

"Let me know when you get here! I want to walk you from your car. The neighborhood can be just a little rough!!!!!"

And then, in my headlights, I saw him. Standing practically in the middle of the street, arms waving overhead under an ancient streetlight with one bulb flickering, Cupido was motioning me to a side parking lot that had seemed hidden on the poorly lit street.

Grateful not to search anymore (either for parking or the bar), I pulled off the street and into the dark unpaved lot. My car was facing what looked like an abandoned warehouse. Only a few other cars had found their way there. Straight ahead were the train tracks, perpendicular to the lot. I was at the end of the world.

Even before I had shut my ignition off, Cupido was at my car door. Beaming, he reached for the handle, opened the door, and looked at me in the nighttime light.

"Wow! You look great," he gushed. "So nice to meet you."

In those first few moments, there was much to take in. For starters, I don't know how Cupido could have ever been heavy. Thin from head to toe, he looked like a pencil, shoulders not much broader than his chest, and his chest the same size as his torso. I wondered if his waist was smaller than mine.

He was standing so close to my door, that as I got out of the car, I had a closeup of his torso, and his skin-tight pink shirt—opened to display "man cleavage" with a completely hairless chest. He looked more like a boy than a man.

Smelling of drugstore men's cologne (a lot of it), Cupido wore a crucifix on a chain around his neck. He had a closely cropped haircut, and his hands were small with manicured nails. His khaki pants were starched and pressed, and his nubuck shoes, while dated, were neat and cared for. His look gave the distinct impression of trying very, very hard to impress.

"Let's go in!" he said. "The bar across the street is such a great place. The wine is delicious, and you'll like the food too. What's your favorite meal? And come to think of it, what's your favorite television show?"

Not at all sure which question to answer, I just smiled and said: "So much to discover. Let's save these fascinating topics for that drink."

Walking into Lorenzo's House, I realized I had seen places like this only in gangster movies. A no-frills sports bar was a throwback in time. This was a neighborhood joint, where people not from the hood were outsiders.

Dimly lit, the long room was all wood. The bar was to the left, with small televisions mounted above it, none tuned to the same channel, and every one of them with volume cranked up loud. The bartenders wore all black, yelling orders to the kitchen over their shoulders. The adjacent dining area was narrow and furnished with basic wooden tables. I already knew the chairs would be uncomfortable.

Cupido seemed perfectly delighted with the setting. After being ignored for at least ten minutes by the harried staff, he ushered me to a small table in the very back of the room. A television hung directly above our heads. I sat looking out into the room. He faced me and the wall.

"Perfect!" he said. "Now I just get to look at you! What would you like to drink? You'll really like the red wine!"

"Yes, that sounds good," I answered, wondering whether I should suggest a snack to go with it.

With repeated failed attempts to catch the eye of a waitress, Cupido finally headed to the bar where he stood for a very long time. Then it hit me. This wasn't his place. He just wanted it to be.

Cupido was gone long enough for me to check out the surroundings. I was one of the few women in the place. Mostly it was single men, or small groups of men, who all leaned into their conversations as if they were keeping life or death secrets. They were here to spend Friday's paycheck, make deals, and maybe pay off debts.

Even though he wasn't one of them, no one was happier to be there than Cupido.

He returned minutes later carrying two small, plain wine glasses. They contained a very dark, cloudy liquid.

"Cheers!" he said, as he placed a glass in front of me on the red and white checked paper placemat. He grinned a grin so wide it made my jaw hurt. "Isn't this great?" he effused.

I nearly spit out the first sip of wine. So bitter, it made my tongue curl, and my taste buds seize up. Lorenzo's house brand won the prize as the most rank wine I had ever tasted.

Grateful that he didn't notice my reaction, I mastered the art of holding the glass to my lips without really drinking. Not really paying attention, Cupido peppered me with questions:

- How is the date so far?
- Do I look like what you imagined?
- Do you go to Mass?
- What is your favorite thing to do on a Friday night?
- Do you think I have an accent?
- Do you like to cook?
- What would you make for a picnic lunch?
- Do you get cold?
- What do you dream about?
- Have you ever seen a train switching station?

To that last one, I had my first ready answer. "No! But I would love to!"

"Well, you are in luck," Cupido said excitedly. "Just across the tracks, there is a station I can show you. How about right now?!"

Thrilled to be getting out of Lorenzo's with only a quarter of my glass of wine consumed, I willingly agreed.

Taking my hand as we left the bar, Cupido led me across the dark street, past the empty and boarded up warehouses, to a footpath I hadn't yet noticed. Up and over a pedestrian walkway bridge above the tracks, he guided me to the other side.

And although it was dark, the lights of an oncoming train beneath us revealed the structure we were about to visit. Perched on what looked like stilts, the concrete block building was accessible only by a poorly lit staircase leading up to a metal door with a small glass window.

After we climbed the stairs, I could just see in the pale light, a tattered paper sign posted on the wall by the door.

NO ADMISSION! it proclaimed.

"Don't worry about THAT!" Cupido said proudly. "I have my badge!"

He pulled open the heavy metal door which creaked loudly on its hinges. A second stairwell ahead wasn't lit at all, and the air smelled like stale coffee. "You okay?" Cupido asked, as he turned his phone flashlight on so we could make our way.

I had no choice but to grip his hand tightly as we ascended a flight of steep stairs, and then another higher one at the turn. Finally, I was relieved to see light ahead of us. It came through another small window in another metal door at the top of the stairs.

Cupido knocked. No response. He knocked again. Still no response. Finally, on the third attempt, a disembodied intercom voice called out:

"Who's there?"

"Hello, I am a train engineer for the LIRR," Cupido said. "I am here with a lady friend to show her around."

The door ahead creaked open and a large man wearing a blue uniform shirt and jeans was backlit against the open door.

"Who are you again?" The man sounded more irritated than concerned about trespassers.

Cupido puffed himself up to his full height and answered: "Here's my badge. This is Kate, my lady friend. She really likes trains."

Gazing at us quizzically, the man shrugged and ushered us through the door. Once we were inside, he looked me up and down, and said:

"Well, well, we never had one as pretty as you at this hour to talk about riding the rails."

Determined to transform this quirky and unexpected circumstance into a memorable outcome, I smiled and said: "Well then, I better take advantage of tonight. This is a once in a lifetime opportunity for me to learn from you!"

For the next hour, I watched fascinated as computer monitors lit up when trains entered and exited the station. I didn't hold back my questions. The more I inquired, the more interested the station-master was in explaining every nuance of how trains were dispatched and switched.

About forty-five minutes in, he said: "You know I have been married for thirty years, and my wife doesn't know one thing about my work. She has never asked me any of the questions you have!" And with that, he slapped Cupido on the back, nearly knocking him over. "You got a live wire here!"

Cupido beamed. "I know, I know. Isn't she great?!"

At the close of an hour, there was a shift change. That was our cue to leave. This time the trip down the stairs was far less precarious. There was a light for the stairs after all, and we had curried enough favor to have it switched on for our departure.

Back outside the clanging door at the base of the stairs, and under a harsh overhead security light which flashed on, Cupido pulled me towards him and kissed me. It was the softest, most gentle kiss.

And then I knew he was a smoker. The telltale scent of his breath mixed with the drugstore cologne caused me to take an involuntary step back and gulp for air.

"Oh, did I scare you?" he said. "I promise to go at your speed. But there is just one thing you should know," he gulped. "I am separated, not divorced. But I swear, it's going to happen. I don't want to lose you."

"Thank you, Cupido," I said. "You didn't scare me. It's past midnight and I must go home."

He walked me back across the tracks to the parking lot and stood beside me as I unlocked the car door. As I leaned into the car, he gave me a quick peck on the cheek and then stood watching as I backed my car out of the deserted lot. Hoping to avoid nails or broken glass underneath my tires, I was slow to pull away.

Cupido came running after me and tapped on my driver's window just as I reached the edge of the lot on the street. I didn't put my window down . . . just waved goodbye, as I heard him yelling:

"This is the start of something great! I will call you tomorrow!"

Even before I made it home, my phone lit up with a text from him:

"I just walked in my door. I mean, I just floated in my door!!!! I had a wonderful evening. Thank you, Cupido."

I didn't answer.

The next morning at 6 AM, my phone lit up again:

"Good morning, Kate. I woke up thinking about you and last night. It was beautiful. It seemed like everything fell into place. I'm getting some things together for dinner with my girls. As for an Italian dinner for you, just say the word and I would love to make you a meal that you will never forget. And if you ever need a bathroom in Penn Station, I have a good one you can go to. I know you are busy today and have a lot to do. I'm free to talk from 3:45 to 4:15, 5:30 to 6:30, 7:45 to 8:15; 9:30 to 10:30, and any time after 11:30. If you get board [sic] and just want to talk I would love to hear from you. If not, no problem. If I don't hear from you, have a great day!!!!"

And for ten days straight, Cupido sent me his work schedule, seeking an opportunity to say hello again. He begged for a phone call. Finally, we spoke.

"I enjoyed meeting you," I began. "But you need to settle your life. I am just beginning to figure mine out. There is a lot that happens between being separated and getting divorced. I moved here to New York to begin again. I am just starting to date, to enjoy meeting new people, and to build my community. I don't plan to get involved. And honestly, I am not comfortable seeing anyone who is not divorced. But we can always be friends," I consoled him.

"Does that mean I can cook for you? Will you meet me in Penn Station?" Cupido pressed. "I would like to give you a tour and introduce you to the stationmaster. And I can show you that bathroom!!!!"

"Yes, we can be friends," I answered. "And maybe someday it will work out for me to take that tour."

The floodgates were open. Every few days, I would get texts at all hours.

"Hello, Kate. Just thought I would send you a little hello just to tell you that I was thinking about the other evening we shared!!!! Hope you are enjoying yourself and not working too much!!!! Cupido."

"I appreciate your being so persistent," I finally answered after my inbox was overrun. "But I need to back away. I am seeing other people, and your situation as it is really doesn't make sense for me. You're a wonderful guy and I so enjoyed the time with you. I do hope you understand."

"Kate!!!!" Cupido pleaded. "Maybe if you could meet some of the guys at Penn Station and the stationmaster you would change your mind!!!"

"Alright, Cupido. I would love a tour,' I conceded. "But that doesn't mean I am going to change my mind. I am traveling for a week. I'll let you know when I get back."

The greeting card arrived while I was gone. As if he had marked his calendar for the exact day I would return, Cupido sent a text very early the next morning:

"Kate, I want to thank you for being honest with me. That says a lot about the type of person you are!!!!! I understand what you mean and can understand where you are coming from. I had a great time with you last month and hope that we may cross paths again in the future. Is there any way I might be able to just give you a call tonight? I would just like to say so long in person and not over a text. No pressure, I'm not going to try to get you to change your mind. I just want to talk to you one more time. I'm leaving my sister's house soon and will be home at 10:00. I still want to show you the control room!!! Please let me. Cupido." (Followed by five train emojis.)

"Hi, Cupido. I can't talk tonight, but let's do this. You tell me your schedule and I will meet you at Penn Station. As long as you understand that we are just friends, I would love for you to show me around."

"Yes, yes, I promise," he said.

Who could resist getting an insider's view of the inner workings of the largest commuter train station in the United States? Built for 200,000 daily commuters, but accommodating 650,000, there are more passengers moving through Penn Station each day than all three of the New York City area major airports. Penn Station is a small city with hordes of people, 21 tracks for commuter and Amtrak trains, restaurants, stores, pop-up vendors, and impromptu musical performances showcased in the convoluted network of hallways and gates.

I arranged to accept Cupido's offer the next week during a work trip through Penn Station. Meeting me when I arrived at Track 21, he looked official in his LIRR uniform and conductor's cap. When

I stepped off the train, he gave me as giant a hug as his small size allowed.

Ushering me through the maze of back hallways away from the public, he guided me into a utilitarian staff lounge where uniformed engineers played card games and talked loudly on their cell phones. When we stepped through the door, they all stopped in unison, surprised to see a woman in a dress standing in their private space.

Cupido proudly announced to all: "This is Kate, my lady friend."

"Hi, everyone," I acknowledged the group, not discrediting his incorrect introduction. They looked up as a group, puzzled but intrigued.

I couldn't help but smile as the tour continued to the secret staff bathroom, where henceforth Cupido said I would have access. That offer was the most beneficial outcome of a first date that never merited a second.

On we went to the grand prize—access to the stationmaster's quarters. Buried deep in the station's bowels, the windowless rooms of the command center were illuminated by wall-to-wall banks of computer screens. It was a vast bunker hidden away under the main concourse where the entire train grid map was displayed on a colorfully lit gigantic console. Focused traffic control staff never took their eyes off the grid nor moved from their positions. Wearing headsets and security clearance badges, they barked out instructions. It was orderly pandemonium. I loved every minute.

With innocent bravado, Cupido approached the stationmaster, introducing me in one long sentence. "Sorry to bother you, sir. This is Kate from Texas who just moved to New York. She is my lady friend. I wanted you to meet her." The stationmaster extended his hand and offered a sincere welcome.

"Few people get to see this control room when we are working. But Cupido is a good man. I am glad he brought you here. Welcome to New York. Come back anytime!"

Outside on the sidewalk, I hailed a taxi.

"Thank you, Cupido," I said, giving him a quick kiss on the cheek as I ran to the car. "You have made my day."

"Oh, no," he answered. "You've made mine. The guys will never stop talking about this one."

Every trip I made into Penn Station after that day reminded me of being treated like royalty by Cupido. Being an insider had only been possible because he was my friend.

All he ever needed in life was chocolate, Cupido had said. Better than Lorenzo's red wine, I knew.

But nothing is as good as learning about the top secret staff bathroom at Penn Station. I never took advantage. All the same, I know where it is. And I won't ever tell.

ANDERSON the Actor

♫ There's No Business Like Show Business ♫

Artist: Irving Berlin

"I like your profile and your spunk," he texted. "Would you meet me for a drink or dinner, or both?"

Anderson had found me online and told me later that what attracted him most was a photo of me wearing a giant Vegas headdress.

That photo had been a "seize the moment" experience at a New Year's Eve party. I was gratified it captured Anderson's attention.

"You look like you just strutted across a stage! Where's your boa and peacock fan?" he continued. "Do explain."

It had been my first New Year's Eve in New York. Friends were producing a mega-concert dance party with magic and Cirque du Soleil acts, and with an into-the-wee hours full-service bar to serve hundreds. They invited me to come. I had arrived in a shiny metallic black dress and fishnet hose. When I had chosen my outfit for the evening, it seemed festive enough.

But once I saw the beautifully costumed crowd, I knew I looked far too ordinary for the likes of this group. A glittery affair, the floor show featured a scantily clad cast in showy sequined costumes. What I found riveting was their incredible plumed head gear. With a strong margarita for fortification, I worked myself backstage to the dressing rooms to "borrow" one of the amazing headpieces from my friends who were staging the production.

No sooner had the enormous plume of gold and black feathers been clamped tightly atop my head did it register I couldn't walk AND balance it at the same time. As I teetered under the weight, I realized I must have photographic proof of the moment.

I smiled wanly for the iPhone snap and then begged a backstage staffer to release me from my misery. Even after the headdress came off, my head hurt for the next two hours.

But Anderson had seized on the photo, and there was finally gain for the pain.

"So nice to see this . . . a charming and interesting woman who isn't afraid to go big. I like that!" he exclaimed.

We arranged a late Monday evening phone call when our schedules both had openings. Even though it was almost 11 PM, I was immediately drawn to the energy of Anderson's broadcaster announcer voice, simultaneously warm and commanding, without being practiced or showy.

"Hello," he began. "Is this the charming showgirl from NYC?! You know, you really should be on the stage."

"I'll be honest with you," I laughed. "If I told you I had worn that getup for more than ten minutes, I would be seriously exaggerating. I'm not cut out for Vegas!"

"Let me be the judge of that," he said. "One of my hobbies is acting . . . so I come by my knowledge of who looks convincing in front of an audience from experience."

Within a few moments, it wowed me to learn that not only was Anderson an actor, he was also a competitive ballroom dancer. His day job as a dentist gave not a clue that he spent evenings at theater rehearsals or in the dance studio. I was intrigued. The same guy that does root canals could also sing and dance in front of hundreds on a stage.

When our call ended an hour later, we had plans for dinner that Sunday night before Anderson's trip to Texas for a dance competition. I couldn't wait to hear more about him and said so in a follow-up text.

"You had me at hello," I admitted. "I can't wait to meet you in person!"

"I feel the same way. Thanks for sharing, and I look forward to Sunday evening!! Sleep well!!"

The week crawled. Every other day, I sent a text, sometimes with a snapshot of my activities: travel, conducting a meeting, sharing a story of a crazy experience, or whatever the day might have brought.

In minutes, Anderson would send his own text responses:

"I hope all the visiting and business is going well! Especially the trip to the dentist. Talk soon . . ."

"Travel safely! NASA has cleared you for re-entry!"

"Wow. An elegant and gorgeous woman! If your words at the event were half as good as the photo, you knocked it out of the park! Were you happy with everything?"

"How are you, Kate? Are you making progress? Thanks for sharing that experience. Your writing is compelling. That story should be a movie. Who should play you?"

Anderson's encouragement, spirited communication, and light-hearted humor created a high level of anticipation for our first meeting. He had made a reservation at The Capital Grille somewhat close to me and about an hour from where he lived.

I was driving in to meet him. When I arrived at the restaurant's address, I was in a giant shopping mall, and my GPS had no idea where the actual restaurant was. To add to the confusion, I was already a few minutes late. The culprit was my indecision about what to wear that would look both casual and smart.

"I have been told my casual is not totally casual," I had confessed to Anderson in an afternoon text on the day we were to have dinner.

Besides the look of my clothes, I was guessing at the right height shoe. The photos I had seen of him were headshots. I wondered whether I might be taller.

"Don't know if we have talked about it," I went on in the text. "But how tall are you? I am always sensitive about the height of the shoes I wear."

"Never worry," he answered. "A man loves a woman regardless of her height. I'm 5' 11". Wear the shoes you feel good in . . . but thanks for the consideration."

His answer had arrived right as I headed out the door in a long gray fitted sweater, button-down blouse, slim jeans, and flats. When I learned Anderson didn't object to a taller profile, I took five minutes to race back inside and change into leather boots with a heel. The shoe switch was just enough to throw my punctual arrival off, along with my sense of control.

So when my GPS faltered, there was no chance I would get to the restaurant on time. Normally never flustered with small hiccups related to meeting a first date, not knowing where to go on this particular evening had me breathless.

I drove around the mall twice and finally texted to ask where I should be. Patiently, Anderson explained where the restaurant was, how to find parking, and offered to come outside to wave me towards the entrance.

Minutes later, we saw each other as I approached the front of the restaurant. Lean and smaller in stature than I expected, he was still a commanding presence with radiating confidence, an authoritative stance, and piercing blue eyes I could see as I got closer.

Immediately, Anderson made me feel at ease, giving me a quick hug, holding the door for me, and then guiding me to the maître'd stand. In a mannerly, friendly way, he said to the captain:

"The lady has arrived. Give us a table where I can talk to her and tell her she is beautiful!"

We were ushered into the sophisticated dining area and seated across from each other in a dark wood booth in the center of the room. A fireplace flickered in the corner, and the subdued lighting set a romantic mood.

From the first cocktail through dessert, I was barely aware of the food, delicious though it was. Anderson was a terrific conversationalist, and there was an undeniable spark between us. We laughed and flirted with ease, and the energy was palpable.

Midway through our steaks, he leaned in.

"This rarely has ever happened so quickly. But I am captivated by you. And I just want to say that. You don't have to answer. But I do want you to know."

I felt the heat rise in my cheeks. I was blushing. The compliment was both unexpected and welcome. I smiled. "In return, I'll admit to telling YOU that this is my best first date," I winked.

After dessert, Anderson reached for my hand across the table. "I am sorry this night has to come to an end. But sadly, I have a 6 AM flight in the morning. I doubt I'll sleep much tonight thinking about this evening. But you need to get home. Let me walk you to your car."

Outside, the parking lot was almost empty. I could see my car far in the distance in one direction and his even farther away in the opposite direction. Quickly surveying the scene, he took my hand and said:

"Come on, let's go. I'm driving you to your car."

Guessing it was a calculated move to get me in his car, I said: "Interesting decision. You must want me to see what you drive!"

"Not at all. I just want to spend a few more minutes with you."

Anderson walked me around to the passenger side of his black BMW, opened the door, and made sure I was comfortably seated. We drove to my car, and he pulled up alongside it.

"Before you get out," he said, "I just must do this." He leaned over and gave me a soft, long, very gentle kiss on the lips. "Ah, there will most certainly need to be more of that!" he said, as he pulled away and looked at me intently. It felt like several silent minutes passed.

Finally breaking his gaze, Anderson pulled on the handle of his door, got out, walked around to my side of the car, and opened my door. Offering me his hand, he assisted me out of the car and patiently waited as I got my keys and opened the driver's side door.

Almost in passing he said very quietly:

"An amazing night."

Back home, I was the first to text.

"Anderson, thank you so much for being persistent to make this first date happen. It far exceeded my expectations, and I must say I had high expectations. You're charming, funny, entertaining, humble, kind, and engaging. I'm just glad I am not your dental patient because it would be against the rules to have a second date! Safe travels tomorrow to my state. Good luck with the dance competition and keep the photos and videos coming!"

His answer arrived twenty minutes later.

“Just walked in my door. You’re welcome and thank YOU! You are a truly beautiful woman, inside and out! I eagerly look forward to our next encounter! In the meantime—videos and photos will be sent your way!

Enjoy the rest of the night and sleep well. I’m not sure I can, however. But I’m not sorry in the least. Life is about living, not sleeping.”

Throughout the week of his travels in Texas, Anderson sent messages:

“Enjoy the day, Kate! Beautiful out this morning here.”

“What are you up to today? Whatever is on your agenda, you’ll nail it.”

“Hope the night is treating you well. Looking forward to seeing you.”

Several weeks later, our second date was an opportunity for me to see Anderson in full on acting mode. He was playing a lead in the musical *Cabaret* at a regional theater on Long Island, about an hour and a half from Manhattan.

Our plan was for me to drive out for the Sunday matinee and then have dinner following the performance. Although I left early enough to make the long drive with time to spare, somehow once again, my GPS failed me. I had landed in an adjoining town, and it was only fifteen minutes until curtain. I frantically texted Anderson about my predicament.

Even though he was ready to step on the stage, he responded. With incredible calmness, Anderson answered: “Don’t worry. You’ll get here when you get here. I just want you to be safe.”

I tore up the roads to the town where I was supposed to be,

screeched into the packed parking lot of the theater, found the last space, and raced into the building. The lobby doors to the theater were closed. I frantically ran to the box office and breathlessly asked the lone attendant for my ticket. She smiled knowingly: "You came from Manhattan, didn't you?"

"Yes!" I gulped, thanking her as I grabbed the envelope, and sprinted into the darkened theater.

It took my eyes a moment to adjust. All I could make out were the backs of rows and rows of heads. Luckily, the curtain was still down. I was the very last person arriving for the show.

Taking a deep breath, I proceeded down the aisle and slid into my seat as if nothing were out of the ordinary. Trying to calm my pounding heart and jagged breath, I glanced at the couple next to me, smiled, and opened my program.

Anderson was perfectly cast as a German commandant. With a self-taught accent, he embodied the role of a serious, authoritative figure cutting purposeful strides across the stage, wearing a dark gray double-breasted suit that fit him impeccably. I particularly delighted in the numbers where he had the chance to sing and dance.

Following the performance, I exited to the lobby where Anderson was waiting with the cast. With each introduction he made of me, I could sense his delight (and maybe even pride) I was there.

Our dinner felt even more romantic than the first one. He spirited me away to a small Italian restaurant with a bustling vibe and a chic feel. This time, we were seated at a corner table where our knees practically touched. I could both see and feel his piercing blue eyes as they fixed on me.

"That perfume you are wearing is carrying me away," he began.

“Oh, and where are we going?” I asked.

“I’ll start here,” he said. And he leaned in to kiss me. “Your lipstick is now my preferred appetizer.”

“It’s number 115,” I disclosed.

“Always a favorite,” he teased.

Just like our first date, the evening flew by. We talked about the show, his village (he promised me a driving tour after dinner), the impending rain shower, AND my lack of an umbrella.

Seeing each other again was going to be a challenge. We lived almost two hours apart in traffic. Planning was going to be important.

“Let’s make the most of the opportunities we do have,” Anderson said. “I like to have experiences and create memories. And I’d like to do that with you.”

And then he added:

“Do you have any fantasies?”

“What kind of fantasies?” I asked.

“The kind you make up. And then make happen. Like stories. Like acting. Like we are characters in a play.”

“Try me out,” I challenged. “I’ll do anything once.”

“Good!” he said, leaning in very closely. And then he whispered in my ear: “You’ll get instructions by text this week.”

Later that evening, Anderson sent me a message:

“Thank you for tonight, for the effort that you made to come out and take a risk on a local production, the uncovering of a few more layers about you, and the knowledge that color 115 lipstick looks good on me! Sleep well, and know that you are in my thoughts, Fraulein! And when you remember which perfume, I want to know.”

The next day, I answered.

"Good morning! I think I know which perfume it is :) Jo Malone. All the scents are wonderful. I'm just not sure what sample I had on."

"We'll just have to do a double-blind study on all the samples you have. Oh, and double-blind studies are always done with wine," he revealed.

"What's better?" I asked. "Perfume or wine?"

"That's not the right question," Anderson answered. "With all due respect, Fraulein, let's try this . . . what do you think of kissing while wearing perfume?"

"Ah, sir, how do YOU see it? I have much to learn . . . ," I countered.

To which he responded:

"Hmmm. To kiss or not to kiss. Kissing to be grateful for the giving and receiving of a gift of beauty and nature, kissing to share in the exploration of another's soul and humanity . . . and of course kissing for the double-blind study of fragrances!!"

"And by the way, I am lying in bed working on some preliminary storyboards for the fantasy scenario I'll be proposing to you," he went on.

"You just conjured up all kinds of images! If I took a wild stab at it, I would say working on storyboards in bed must be decidedly different from working on them in say a dental office with patients in your chair. Maybe I could assume some responsibility here. Why don't I be in charge of the soundtrack?" I offered.

"Yes!!" Anderson came back. "You're absolutely in charge of the soundtrack! You are keeping my imagination active. And now I am supposed to sleep?!"

Early the next morning, he sent me a text:

"I just wanted to say to you that I've been having the time of my life! You are fun, interesting, and extraordinarily charming! And I still smell your perfume and am VERY distracted. Wait for my message!"

Two days later, the fantasy invitation arrived by voice mail:

"Hello. My name is Anderson . . . your number was given to me by a friend. He says you are smart, funny, beautiful and wear the best perfume. I'm hoping you're available tomorrow evening as I will be in Manhattan and am looking for a companion for the evening! Dinner . . . and whatever follows! You come highly recommended!"

I waited until the end of the day to respond.

"Hello, Anderson, I am intrigued. Tell me more."

"I was told you would be a lovely person to spend an evening with. I have a reservation for dinner at the STK Steakhouse Midtown. The address is 1114 Avenue of the Americas, New York. Be there by 7:30 PM. We'll share a drink and get to know one another! I'll be in the bar," he said mysteriously.

"I'll look forward to meeting you," I responded. "Any personal preferences for my attire?"

"Please be comfortable, but I'll ask for feminine. Let me see your attributes . . . I'm a visual man."

"I can already say I'm quite impressed with your selection of meeting locations," I answered. "I'll be certain to wear clothing to meet your expectations. How would you feel about a red dress? Should I call you Anderson, or do you go by Andy?"

"Anderson is fine for now . . ."

This time, I made sure to get to the restaurant early. I wanted to have the lay of the land. Even though I had been out with Anderson, this date scenario felt like a completely novel experience. We were going to pretend we didn't know each other. He was going to pick me up in the bar . . . or I was picking him up. The discovery of how the evening would play out was part of Anderson's fantasy.

When I arrived, there was a buzzing crowd at the entrance and in the bar. STK is a 'see and be seen' scene. With an enormous vaulted ceiling, blue and purple up-lighting on geometric columns flanked by white trees, and cozy leather banquettes in a cavernous space, the restaurant is always jam-packed.

Not spotting Anderson, I worked my way past the throng at the door and claimed a swivel stool at the far end of the bar. Ordering an Aperol Spritz, I felt like I was starring in a "Sex and the City" episode. Wearing a form fitting red lace dress, pearls, and heels, I had made certain to choose Jo Malone perfume.

With legs crossed, I turned my body towards the center of the room to survey the crowd. The tips of my shoes brushed the metal footrest of the barstool, and the lace hem of my dress grazed my legs above the knees. I was a character in this show, ready for what came next.

So absorbed was I in people watching, I hadn't realized that Anderson had come up behind me. I felt a hand on my shoulder and a soft kiss on my neck. "Hello, M' Lady. You must be Kate. You look lovely! I can't wait to spend the evening together."

And from that moment on, we never broke out of our roles. I was the woman who had come to the steakhouse to meet a stranger. And that stranger was there to seduce me.

It was a deliciously naughty evening. The food was the finest red meat, and the red wine kept flowing. The sophisticated crowd hummed all around us. We flirted and pretended and acted our parts.

At the end of the evening, Anderson paid the bill, took my hand across the table, and broke the spell.

"I have something to tell you," he said. "I'll be me now. I've always wanted to have an evening like this, and you were the perfect person to be with.

But I can't go through with it. I'm falling in love with you, and I know that I shouldn't. We live too far apart, and I am sure that you deserve more than someone who can only see you every few weeks. I have thought about this nonstop. But I don't see any other way."

The tears welled up in my eyes, and without warning, one slipped down my cheek and landed on the v-shaped décolletage of my red dress.

"I think I understand," I said. "But this is not the ending that I anticipated for our evening."

"Yes, I know," he said. "Nor for me either."

Anderson called me a car, and we stepped outside, holding hands, saying nothing. He put me in the Uber and gently shut the door. Just as the driver moved away from the curb, rain began to fall. I could not look back. The entire ride home, I replayed the evening in my head.

When I walked into the apartment, I kicked off the heels, removed my pearls, and sat to regain my composure. Then I sent a message:

"Anderson, there's much I want to say, and I don't want to let the moment pass. You are very special to me and we only get these gifts of heart, mind, and chemistry in rare circumstances. So, expect I will stay in touch, and that I want to remain a friend. I feel like someone put ice in all my veins. But I trust you know what you are doing."

Anderson's long answer comforted me:

"I'm so sad tonight . . . I had eager anticipation of exploring a life with you. With your obvious beauty, class, intelligence, warmth, sensuality . . . your easy laugh, and your interest in others! But most importantly was the impact you've had on me . . . You showed me that love is possible, that I'm someone to love and care about!

But it's all about the timing and how you deserve so much more than we were going to have. You deserve the world and knowing you, you will get it! Go get that next big thing. I am and always will be on your side, available to help you in any way. I love you, Anderson."

Over time, I came to terms with what could never have been. Anderson was right. I needed to find a Manhattan match.

True to my promise. Anderson and I are still friends. Good friends.

And when I see him, I always wear Jo Malone perfume.

MACK the Matchmaker

♫ Don't Stop Believin' ♫

Artist: Journey

When I first got to New York, figuring out how to meet people—friends, work colleagues, men to date—in a strange (and mammoth) new community was an ever-present challenge. But I was determined to be open to all the possibilities.

After a few months of online dating, I was recounting my frustrations in a phone call to my happily partnered up sister in the South. "Ninety percent of the men I find on these sites aren't really my type," I told her. "I rule them out in a flash when I see their selfies. The photos are all so predictable: behind the steering wheel of a car, wearing sunglasses, with their seat belts covering their upper torso. Or the familiar closet mirror pose with an unmade bed in the background. Or the gym shot, flexing arm muscles, bench pressing heavy weights overhead. Or the absolute worst combination: posing with a giant fish, while chomping on a cigar."

"Why not sign up for a matchmaking service?" she laughed. "I hear they weed out the undesirables and have a lock on all the "good guys" who would never go online."

"There's got to be a hefty price tag," I told her.

"Investigate it," she said. "It might be worth it if it saves you the scary selfie guys and turns up a wonderful man. What are you willing to pay to find the right guy and reclaim your time?"

After scouring online for a company that seemed legit, I found a site that called itself an exclusive club. The first step was completing a digital application on my match preferences.

What age range? Race/ethnicity? Religion? Education level?

Occupation? Height/Body type? Prior marital status? With or without children? Interest in marriage and having children? Most important quality in a partner? Distance willing to travel? Any deal breakers?

Within a week of submitting an application and the required five photos, it was time for step two. I had advanced to a phone interview. Yvette, the club representative who called, was young, upbeat, and enthusiastic.

She started off with club statistics: 10,000 members and 50 staff.

"New York City is our headquarters," she said, "but we have offices around the globe. You can trust that we have great outreach. Here are the cities and areas where we find the most members and do the most matches," she revealed:

New York
Los Angeles
Chicago
Houston
Miami
London
Geneva
Côte d'Azur

Fifteen minutes into the call, Yvette announced I had "been approved" to meet with a matchmaker. Even though I was permitted to join the Club, no matches would be made until I paid my yearly dues. Both men and women pay, she had told me. But men pay more, and are willing to do so, to find the most desirable women.

I was told to wire a partial payment to an LLC, with a different name than the Club. Once that deposit check cleared the bank, the Club staff scheduled a meeting with a matchmaker.

"Would you like a male or female?" Yvette asked. "Male," I responded, curious to get a man's perspective on the level of interest single men might have in me.

A week later, matchmaker Mack emailed me, suggesting we meet at the lobby bar of the Grand Hyatt Hotel attached to the Grand Central Terminal train station. His message was friendly enough. But his mistake-filled communication triggered my first alarm bell.

> Hi Kate
>
> My name is Mack and I am going to be doing your
>
> inperson Consultation.
>
> Does this thursday, nov 30th at 2:00 pm at the Grand Hyatt
>
> Cafe work for you.
>
> Look forward to meeting
>
> Thanks
>
> Mack
>
> Read more here . . .
>
> The Club, Elite Dating Service
>
> Matchmaking and Dating for those accustomed to Excellence

The day of our meeting, Mack emailed to say traffic was going to make him a few minutes late. It was clear his writing style was not improving.

> Hi Kate
>
> My train is a bit late. Probably be there around 210.

> Sorry bout delay
>
> Sent from my iPhone

By the time Mack showed up twenty minutes late, the thought had crossed my mind that maybe this entire operation was a sham. But then he arrived, looking professional enough in tailored slacks, a cardigan, and a button-down shirt. In his mid-50s, he carried a briefcase and reminded me of the men I was accustomed to seeing in the business world. So, I dismissed the thought.

I was sitting in the upstairs bar at a small table in the center of the room, drinking water, and reviewing my notes for a work presentation I was to give that night. Because I was speaking to a large gathering at the New York Yacht Club, I was wearing a dressy black knit pantsuit that could work for the evening meeting, and then for a dinner date afterward.

Mack came over to join me. Was it my imagination, or did Mack have an initial look of discomfort? What was going through his mind? Was I not the typical "client"? Did my work attire label me as someone who was more business than not?

Mack sat down, offered me something else to drink, and took out his notepad. He began on an encouraging note. There were many intelligent, attractive single men in New York that belonged to the Club. They preferred not to go online and were too busy to meet women without the assistance of the Club staff.

"You definitely have the credentials to interest them," Mack said conspiratorially.

"Oh! Why is that?" I asked, surprised by his comment.

"I know," he responded quickly. "Let's just say I have seen too many New York women who act entitled. You come across as being the opposite." He twisted his wedding ring as he spoke.

"Guys like women who create their own happiness; guys are attracted to confidence. 'She who is the most certain always wins!'"

Mack went on:

"Your date will focus on what he feels when he is around you: fun, adventure, anticipation. And this can be addictive. You are mysterious and surprising. An interesting and thrilling high-value woman is so appealing."

"We will have you matched in no time. I can promise you will be delighted by the men we can introduce to you. Our service promises to give you three high-quality matches in a year. You will receive them one at a time. We won't match you with the second person until you tell us you are not satisfied with the first match."

"We take our time to get just the right fit. I'm going to write a profile of you from our meeting today and then we will use it to find the perfect man who matches yours."

"What if I don't like the matches?" I asked.

"I promise we will keep going until you do," Mack said reassuringly.

"One important point," I said, as we concluded. "I want to meet people who live in New York."

Mack nodded his understanding and hastily made an entry on his notepad.

After our meeting, I emailed Mack to say thanks. He replied:

> Yes, it was very nice meeting you as well. I think you are a very interesting special person and look forward to helping you meet someone wonderful
>
> Thanks so much
>
> Mack

A week later, Mack emailed me a summary of my match preferences based on the questions we had reviewed in our meeting. The responses he attributed to me were far off the mark. Every answer he claimed I gave was the opposite of what I had said. Mrs. Brown, my fierce and memorable 8th grade English teacher, would have had a field day with the way he wrote.

Question: What occupation for prospective matches?
Mack's recall of my preference: "No high-profile men"
What I actually said: I want to meet successful men with ambition.

Question: Prior marital status?
Mack's recall of my preference: "Never married no good"
What I actually said: They need to be divorced. Beyond that, it doesn't matter.

Question: Interest in marriage?
Mack's recall of my preference: "Marriage"
What I actually said: I have no plans to get married again.

Question: Distance willing to travel?
Mack's recall of my preference: "Most everywhere but Texas"
What I actually said: I do not want to travel anywhere to meet matches.

Also attached was the profile of me Mack had written. Filled with misspellings, typos, punctuation errors, and factual inaccuracies, it was laughingly incorrect and disappointingly simple. I was especially shocked since Mack had appeared to be paying attention and taking pages of notes in our two-hour meeting together.

> Kate is the epitome of style, sophistication and elegance. She has a classic external beauty is matched by her wonderful kind and caring disposition. Born in the south she radiates a that anti-bellum type charm but has the drive and energy of a modern woman. She has embraced all of NYC has to offer. She loves so walk and explore, travel, work out, take yoga classes as well as watch many sports especially football. Kate always is impeccably dressed for any occasion whether attending a black-tie even or a casual day she will catch anyones eye. Kate tirelessly help those in need and really cares deeply for her heart. Kate is true combination of beauty, class and kindness.

I emailed back immediately.

> Mack, if you don't mind, I am going to take a stab at writing a profile that better defines me.

Mack responded in a now predictable, oddly written, and poorly punctuated answer:

> Hi Kate
> Of course make any changes you wish. I really liked it felt it was truly you
> Sent from my iPhone

My response was measured:

> Hi, Mack,
> I appreciate your giving it your best shot. There are some basic concepts about who I am that I want to communicate. Thanks for giving me the chance to make

> those changes. I'll get it back to you next week.
>
> Kate

Mack's response was quick:

> Yes very much you that is true. Of course it wont do justice to the Kate Somerset in person"
>
> Sent from my iPhone

When Mack got my changes—which amounted to an almost entirely rewritten profile—he answered back:

> Good am well this barely resembles what I wrote but I love it. I will send it on. The tech people will edit it etc. and fit it to a profile
>
> I will let you know as a finished product
>
> Thanks
>
> Mack

With my new profile submission now in hand, Mack went on to say that all he needed was confirmation I had made the final Club dues payment. Then matching could begin. A second alarm bell rang in my head. I had already paid. I emailed him immediately.

> Mack, happy Monday. Just wanted you to know I wired the money for the balance owed two weeks ago.
>
> Thanks much.
>
> Kate

Mack's answer set off the third alarm bell.

> Hi, Kate
>
> Great news thanks for letting me know. im sure you did.

> Once they let me know it hits I will send your match pref
> docs and sample profile
> Very excited to get started
> Thanks

A MONTH later, Mack sent me the sample of my full profile. Although it contained the copy I had written, the photo placement was completely botched. Instead of including the five photos the Club required I send, it contained only two. And of the two, one was used twice . . . on the same page.

I contacted Mack immediately and asked for an explanation.

> Thats sometimes how they create them. Other than that
> your up and ready to have prospective matches
> Very excited for you to get started
> Sent from my iPhone

It wasn't worth arguing the point about my photos. I wanted to focus on matches. TWO MONTHS had now passed since my initial meeting with Mack.

Then ANOTHER month later, Mack sent me an email about the first potential match.

> Hi Kate
> hope you are doing well. I have a very interesting fun
> gentleman who would like to meet you His name is
> Howard and he is in NYC this wknd. Let me know if you
> have interest and I will make the arrangements

I read the profile. Howard lived in California. His headshot photo showed a serious, unsmiling man, with a long beard, half white and half gray. With his dark receding hair, very thick dark eyebrows, and his dark sunken eyes, he looked lifeless and spooky. This was not the match for me.

> Hi, Mack,
>
> My life is crazy booked, so when I do get the chance to meet someone new, I need a bit more notice. You gave me two days. Also, you know I want to meet someone in New York. California doesn't work for me and my geographic preferences.

Mack responded:

> Hi Kate
>
> he is at present a semiNew Yorker being here half the time Yes It was short notice on our end which is not the normal process. He will be returning soon when I have his dates I will let you know speak to you soon.
>
> Thanks
>
> Mack
>
> Sent from my iPhone

I wasted no time responding.

> Mack, thanks. Honestly, it doesn't matter when he's coming back. His looks don't really appeal to me. I have asked you to find a full-time New Yorker. Have a great weekend. Thanks so much.

Mack's answer was quick:

> Beauty is in the eye of the beholder. Who am i to say what someone might think is good looking or not. Now if I was a lady such as you, no i would doubt you find him attractive,

of course that is hypothetical

LOL

Sent from my iPhone

Days went by.

Weeks went by.

With an even louder fourth alarm bell sounding in my head, I sent Mack an email in frustration:

RE: The Texan and Radio Silence

Hi, Mack,

How are you? Long time, no speak!

Did you know it's been more than four months since I handed over my trust and money to your Club? What's happening for the Texan that you thought would be so successful in NYC?

True, I'm dating a lot, but still waiting for Prince Charming!

Any updates?

Have a great weekend!

Kate

When Mack answered back, he misspelled my name.

Hi Katee

yes I am well. yes Im aware and I am in contact with a number of potential matches so just working out some logistics. I had a couple of gentleman interested in meeting you but they resided in your previous home state so that was a no go.

I'll be back shortly with some very nice matches for you.

Hope you are well.

Mack

I answered, by now not meaning a word:

> Thanks so much! Yes, no Texans allowed! I moved to New York and I am here to stay. As always, please give me as much notice as possible. I have to shove the other guys off the calendar. Just kidding.
>
> Have a great day, Mack.
>
> Kate
>
> PS Remember no more scary eyes, bad beards, or frightening ties like the guy from California :)"

Still defending Howard, Mack wrote back:

> LOL hes a sweetheart. But ok got it
>
> Sent from my iPhone

Another MONTH went by. Mack sent me an email:

> RE: High quality match
>
> Hi Kate
>
> hope our Northeast snow didnt get to you too much lol
>
> I have a very nice fun gentleman who is interested in meeting you
>
> R is an extremely attractive, clearheaded, balanced gentleman. He is mentally, physically, and emotionally strong, reliable and masculine. R. is also elite and refined. Highly educated and successful (only works because he wants to not because he has to), R. holds an MBA from an Ivy League University. R. also enjoys the arts from fine art to music and more. If you prefer a handsome, intelligent, successful gentleman who is as optimistic and clear-headed as they get, R. is perfect for you. R. in 3 words:

> attractive, strong, reliable.
>
> Let me know he will be around in mid april
>
> Very exciting
>
> Thanks
>
> Sent from my iPhone

With a kernel of hope, I answered:

> Thanks, Mack. Looks more promising! Where does he live? Any photos?

Mack responded promptly:

> He's in CT and NYC but away for a bit. That's why mid april
>
> not sure on the photos but will check.
>
> You are in high demand all over.

Two weeks went by. Then Mack sent one blurry photo of a man wearing a ski helmet. All I could see of the face were his eyes.

Beyond exasperated, I sent Mack a message:

> Mack, checking back with you. It will be almost five months next week since we met. I'm beginning to question the validity of my decision to turn over my hard-earned funds for a process that works so slowly.
>
> You say you might have a person for me to meet next month. But you can't produce a photo. He's away and will be available only on April 22. None of it adds up.
>
> My alarm bells are loudly clanging. Let's just say I can't recommend your Club to anyone at this point. If you want to disabuse me of the notion that the Club is not a great deal, please do. Others I've spoken to about my dealings

with you, especially in New York City, are equally skeptical.

Hope you have a good weekend.

Kate

Amazingly, this got Mack's attention.

Hi, Kate,

If you would like to speak please give me a call at my office around three or let me know what is a good number to call you

Sent from my iPhone

Several more weeks passed as Mack made two half-hearted attempts to reach me, leaving messages at odd times of the day and then not returning my calls. I sent another email.

Mack, your last email about my concerns was three weeks ago. Other than a brief one-sentence email response, you haven't made any real attempt to resolve them. And I've been very busy since I emailed you. I am moving to a new apartment in NYC and don't have time to keep chasing you down.

It has been six months since we met. So far, the only "quality matches" I've gotten have been with men who don't live here, except one who does, whose only picture is in a helmet.

Now I have to believe two things:

1) The Club takes money but never delivers, and,

2) You must have to take medication to sleep at night over promises unfulfilled.

I'm thinking seriously about writing an article for the

New York Times about the dangers of membership dating services like yours. Given the costly and poor experience I have had with you, I feel it's really incumbent on me to warn others.

One of the most important values in my life is delivering on my word. It's discouraging that there are business models like the Club's which operate in such an unsatisfactory way. You're a nice guy, so why are you involved in this ridiculousness?

Kate

Mack answered me back in a lighting flash.

Kate,

Nice to hear from you. Congrats on your move in New York City. That will be a slot of fun. Regarding you threat to write a mostly false negative article to the NYT is of course your right. Fair warning you should check your contract to make sure there will be legal repercussions as well as a guaranteed rebuttal from the Club's management

I have several attempts to contact you regarding your concerns three weeks ago but is you who have not been able to respond.

Secondly I don't have your file in front of me but we showed a high-quality match you turned down. We then showed you another match who you agreed to meet who will returning to New York April 22 as we have already told you.

Thirdly since I've spoken to you in the past I believe your comment about me not being able to sleep at night was a sort of funny quip. If not then I strongly suggest that you

> apologize for judging my integrity in this manner
> I want your explanation on this comment so we can move forward
> Thanks
> Mack
> Sent from my iPhone

I took several weeks to answer. But Mack beat me to it. His next email presented me with two more match options. One man lived in DC. The other shuttled between London and Berlin and was too well known to reveal a name or photo. I declined.

Mack countered.

> RE: High-quality matches 2 and 3.
> They are often in NY hence the reason they were presented to you, especially with the busy schedule you. I would entertain meeting one of them because you never know where they might end up living
> Thanks
> Sent from my iPhone

By now, the alarm bells had quit ringing. Each communication from Mack was more a waste of time than a jarring recognition that I had been played the fool.

I began composing the letter to the *New York Times* in my head. My response to Mack was predictably rote:

> Thank you, Mack,
> As much as the latest two might be impressive, they are not residents of New York. I am holding tight to that requirement.

> Thanks for continuing to look. Remember: the moral of the story is I need a New Yorker!
> Kate

Either truly unable to understand, or prone to argue . . . or both, Mack's answer was also defensively predictable:

> Hi Kate
> yes this is true but G is often a nYC visitor as well as you could be in DC.
> T comes to NyC from Europe or you could go here
> But it's up to you.

My answers got shorter.

> No. I am never in DC and I don't plan to go to Europe. I prefer someone living here . . . as I have said.
> Thank you.

The next month, Mack sent a message that I barely glanced at:

> Hi Kate
> I am working on a few and should have something shiny soon lol.

I didn't answer.

A day later, Mack sent a profile.

> Kate, here's the gentleman I was speaking about>His profile is avail. Benjamin is very smart and successful and I would love to meet you. Let me know and I will set it up
> Benjamin is a tall, fit, or refreshingly optimistic gentleman who has a captivating zest for life. He is cultured and

> refined yet or the comment what I can authentic. The first words to come to mind with thinking of Benjamin are: attractive, charming, sincere, uplifting, kind, and engaged in life and all it has to offer. And Ivy League graduate he also played tennis all the way to Nationals. He enjoys producing films and continues to engage in those projects as well. In his free time, Benjamin loves film, theater, dance, hiking, museums . . . And of course Travel! Benjamin is well dressed, sociable and refined. If you prefer a gentleman who loves to laugh and by default sees the bright side of life, then Benjamin is perfect for you! Benjamin in a few words: charming, upbeat, strong (mentally, emotionally etc.) fit.

Surprise, surprise! Benjamin is a New Yorker.

I agreed to meet him.

Because of my move to a new apartment in New York City, I delayed the date for three weeks.

The appointed day came. I had not talked to Benjamin, nor been told his last name or provided any details about how we were to reach each other. All I knew was that the date was at 7:30 PM.

Leaving my home early in the morning, I had to dress for the evening, without knowing the destination or proper attire for dinner with Benjamin. Previously, Mack had told me that the Club handled all date arrangements, and "you are told in 'due time' what they are".

As of 4 PM, I still had zero information.

In almost laughable frustration, I sent a message to Mack:

> How is Benjamin going to get my phone number? We are now inside the four-hour countdown. And I'm headed into

> a meeting, so won't be able to communicate with you or anyone else for another hour at least. Help!

At the end of my meeting, nearly two hours later, I checked my phone. No word from Mack. It was almost 6 PM. The dinner was looking less and less like it was happening.

Not totally surprised by the complete disorganization of this latest episode, I texted Mack again:

> Hi, Mack,
>
> Still looking for Benjamin's phone number . . .
>
> Thanks,
>
> Kate

Mack finally answered.

> As am I.

I fired back.

> Sounds like I should conclude this isn't happening, then?

Five minutes later, Mack responded with a text containing a phone number. Nothing else.

In a complete leap of faith, I texted the number Mack had sent.

> Hi, Benjamin,
>
> Very nice to meet you! I look forward to getting acquainted tonight. Can you tell me where I'm going?

At the same time I was typing a text to him, Benjamin called my cell and left me a message.

Who would have believed it? The date was actually on.

We met at an Upper East Side neighborhood restaurant of Benjamin's choosing. I beat him there and was seated at a microscopically small table. Looking around at the other diners, it was obvious I was overdressed in my sundress and heels. That opinion was quickly confirmed when Benjamin arrived in a T-shirt, jeans, and tennis shoes.

"Sorry, I just got off the tennis court," he apologized. "I don't know what you know about me. I am a tennis pro at a club on Long Island and I needed to race out the door after my last lesson to get to you."

Benjamin was a good conversationalist and dinner was delicious. But after a long day and chasing down Mack for details about the date, the normal energy I would have put into the evening felt lacking. I hoped Benjamin didn't notice.

When dinner was over, he offered to drive me home. Dropping me off, Benjamin said how much he enjoyed meeting me. It had been a pleasant evening.

When I walked in my door, I sent Mack an email.

> Thank you for arranging tonight. Benjamin is a very nice man, but we don't share a lot of common ground. I am not a tennis player and he's an expert. Also, there isn't enough chemistry. So I would like to move on to the next match.
> Thanks much,
> Kate

The following afternoon, Mack answered back.

> oh that's too bad. I would like to have a brief follow-up chat about the date. Let me know you can speak

Yes onward

Thanks

Sent from my iPhone

Our call the next day was brief. By then, Mack had spoken to Benjamin, who indicated he was interested in seeing me again. I responded that while I felt Benjamin was an enjoyable date, he wasn't the match I was looking for.

Mack persisted.

But he thought you were great and really liked you.

Wouldn't you consider going out with him again?

I stood firm.

No, I don't want to lead him on, and I really don't want this to be considered a match by the Club.

Mack sounded annoyed.

He's definitely into you. Suit yourself,

Months passed. Emails from Mack slowed to a trickle. I had almost forgotten about the Club. And then, SIX MONTHS after my dinner date with Benjamin, I heard again from Mack.

Hi, Kate,

Hope you are well. Trying to get caught up with you. Last we spoke B. who I sent a profile of to you was a possiblitly

Let me know

Thanks

Sent from my iPhone

Confused, I sent Mack a message.

> I don't recall getting that profile of anyone named 'B'. Please resend.
>
> Thank you, Kate.

Mack came back:

> Okey-Dokey.
>
> Big tennis player. Here he is . . .

And appearing below was the profile of Benjamin that I had received MONTHS ago for our one-time date.

In shock, I sent Mack a message:

> Mack! Don't you remember? You matched me to Benjamin in May! He's the only match I had through your Club in almost a year. You have surely given up on matching me. But are you still trying to match HIM . . . and with me?! This is so par for the course.
>
> Kate

Mack fired off a response:

> Of course I do. I'm asking if you were interested in meeting him
>
> That was not he only met you were shown. Anyway the length of time to send you matches is by far too long so I agree with you there
>
> Sent by my iPhone

I couldn't believe it. I couldn't resist continuing the email exchange with Mack.

> Yes, of course, I met him. You and I even talked about what I thought of the date. You pleaded with me to go out with him again. Have you not been able to match him with anyone else since then?! Poor guy!
>
> As for my matches, you never showed me anyone from New York BUT Benjamin . . . only people from somewhere else whose travel schedules never really put them in New York. So those weren't even matches.
>
> What I can't believe is the comedic irony of your trying to match me again with the ONLY person you ever introduced me to. Did you also offer to him to match with me . . . again?! How incredibly awkward and disorganized!

Attempting to dig himself out of a ridiculous hole, Mack answered:

> Perhaps I didn't phrase it correctly. I had spoken to him a while back and asked me if you were interested in seeing them again. On occasion we will do that. He liked you alot Your opinion of our level of service and overall Club is not great so a negative comment from you of course was expected. No matter we have a contract so I'll continue to find matches in intros for you.
>
> Thanks,
>
> Mack

I gave it one final shot:

> You had already tried to convince me to go out with Benjamin again. I don't believe for one second that's what you

> were doing this go around, or you would have said so at the outset. You forgot you ever matched us, that we went out, and that you tried very hard to convince me to have a second date with him. How bizarre!
>
> It has now been six months since that one and only date with Benjamin. Unless he contacted you again about me, which I highly doubt, this communication is another example of complete ineptitude on your part. I'm just hoping you didn't show my profile to him again. How embarrassing for you.

Mack's retort was quick:

> no one showed your profile to him again
>
> Sent from my iPhone

All I could do was laugh and call my sister.

"Look what you got me into," I said.

"But you got one date out of it," she countered.

"And you have an unbelievable story if you ever decide to write that article for the *New York Times*!"

MARCUS the Manager

♫ So Far Away ♫

Artist: Carole King

As my aircraft taxied away from the gate at the end of a pre-holiday work trip to Texas, I gave my phone one more cursory look before putting it in airplane mode. Sitting on the plane before takeoff back to New York, I had been idly surfing Bumble, my favorite online dating app.

I had joined a few months after moving to the Northeast, and appreciated the app's design which lets women make the opening comment—always an advantage. It eliminated being messaged by matches who couldn't come up with a more compelling opener than the one word "Hi". Even better, letting me make the first move provided an opportunity to set the tone of the exchange.

As I became more comfortable with my online dating persona through my first New York summer and autumn, I solidified the best opening line for me. With Bumble matches, I started a conversation in one of three ways:

If I was interested, I would be direct in saying so, and then add a call to action.

"Hi, first name. You have a great profile. I particularly liked learning about . . . (I would name something specific the man mentioned and then relate it to my own background.) So, it would be fun to meet you. How can we arrange that?"

If I wasn't sure about my level of interest, I would gauge how smart, communicative, clever, and self-deprecating a man was by his answer to this message:

"Hi, first name. What an interesting profile! What do you like best about yourself?"

And if I matched with a man who lived too far away—but who appeared to be someone I would want to meet otherwise—I would send an "honorable mention" encouragement:

"Hi, first name. Sadly, it appears we are geographically challenged. But I enjoyed reading about you, and just wanted to wish you good luck in finding your girl."

On this sunny December afternoon, as the plane rumbled towards takeoff and wheels up to the Big Apple, my index finger tapped the cover photo of a dating profile . . . and I hesitated.

A tall, well-built, affable looking man, wearing a smart dark gray tuxedo, white boutonniere in his lapel, and standing at least a good foot taller than the young bride on his arm, Marcus from Dallas appeared worth the pause. In each of his additional profile pictures, he had the friendliest of smiles, his eyes twinkled, and he looked genuinely engaged with the camera.

Judging strictly from the photos, this was a sophisticated man with an awareness of the image he wanted to project.

Each photo told the beginning of a story about Marcus that made me want to learn more:

1st picture:
Eating a cupcake from a pastry vending machine
(*What city has those?!*)
2nd picture:
Standing on a picturesque cliff with the ocean in the distance
(*What cliff? What ocean?*)

3rd picture:

Holding a glass of wine, seated on a patio with a flowering trellis behind him. (*His home?*)

4th picture:

Dressed in smart business attire, looking confident outside an office complex. (*His work?*)

5th picture:

Escorting his daughter down the aisle as the handsome father of the bride.

Despite the appeal of the photos, there was a problem. Marcus had recently moved from California to live in Texas; I had recently moved from Texas to live in New York.

As my plane was hurtling down the runway, I hurriedly typed a message:

"Hi, Marcus, I found you on Bumble as I am taking off from DFW today. Our paths are connected for a moment. It looks like you moved to Dallas as I was moving from Texas to NY. Just wanted to say sorry we couldn't meet, and good luck in your search. Happy holidays!"

Then I turned my phone off.

When I landed at La Guardia Airport in New York, I powered my phone back on. Marcus had answered.

"Good afternoon, Kate. I really appreciate you reaching out, even though you have moved to New York. That's a very classy thing to do . . . and unfortunately for me . . . you're exactly the type of girl I'm looking for. Enjoy the holidays in NY. If you're ever back in Texas and need a friend to have a drink with, here's my number."

His area code was California. His emoji was a sweet, understated smile. I sent him a reply.

"Marcus, it's Kate. I just landed in NY. If I had run across your profile a few days earlier, we could have had that drink in Texas. But thanks for your number. I now know where to find you!"

By the time I had collected my baggage, hailed a taxi, and started my hour ride home, Marcus had answered again.

"Hi, Kate—it's Marcus." The smile emoji.

"Hi, Marcus! By the way, I love your name."

"Thanks! My mom says she thought long and hard about it . . ."

"Just put you in my phone as 'Marcus Dallas' . . . bet your mom didn't have to think about your last name!"

"It's Lombardi. I might be a little bit Italian."

"Think?" I countered. "What do you do, Marcus Lombardi?"

"I run a business division for a large national company. Moved here from California in March and love it. But now I may have to consider NY!"

"Hey, I might be worth it! Or at least come see a Broadway show :) Please wear that suit in your last profile picture when you were walking your daughter down the aisle. And bring me a cupcake from that vending machine in your first photo."

Marcus was quick:

"I think you should invite me to come see you, and we will go exploring together. I hear NY has some decent food . . ."

"Well, I've found a few great Italian restaurants," I agreed.

"I'm in," he answered.

"But you'd have to like Broadway!"

"With you, I would," he assured me.

By this time, Marcus and I had swapped cell phone numbers and switched our exchange from Bumble to texting. It was the first step in moving away from the dating app and towards an actual date.

What appeared next on my phone were two photos of Marcus—one in informal attire and the second in business dress. In the first, Marcus wore a golf shirt, sunglasses, and ball cap. The setting appeared to be the driving range of a golf course. In the second shot, he stood in a crowd, presumably at an event, wearing a tailored sports jacket, a white button-down shirt, and dress slacks.

"Two contrasting pics of me. Showing I'm pretty versatile."

"And which is the you today?" I asked. "I'll send you evidence of the two sides of me."

My contrasting photos were both seasonal. In the first, I wore a red and black buffalo check flannel shirt, smiling next to Santa Claus at a Christmas display in a local store. In the second, I was dressed in a Kelly-green satin evening gown, standing in front of an enormous Christmas tree at the New York Yacht Club.

The texting conversation continued throughout my long taxi ride home from the airport.

"Beautiful! How tall are you?"

"5' 7"ish. You?"

"I'm 6' 3"."

"Love tall men and their clothes!" I answered.

"I might have a lot of clothes," he confessed.

"Oh gosh! I might have more than you. Take that back. I definitely have more than you. And let's not talk about shoes," I admitted.

"So, we have to get two extra bedrooms for our clothes and shoes!" suggested Marcus.

The conversation was completely captivating me.

"Is this your street?" asked the taxi driver.

Looking up, confused, I realized I hadn't even known I was close to home.

"Yes," I answered. "I live right here."

As the driver ran my credit card, I typed one more response to Marcus.

"You are a man after my own heart. Just got home. So glad we connected."

Twelve days passed. It was the week before Christmas.

"Guess what?" came a message from Marcus on a Tuesday afternoon at the close of the workday.

"W? H? A? T???" I answered.

"Just thinking about you is all . . ." he said.

"Well, really now, you should do something about that!"

"Under the circumstances, I did the best I could . . . I reached out."

"I give you major points for that!" I said.

"So . . . we're gonna work on a points system . . . ok," Marcus challenged.

"You are making me laugh!" I said. "So how am I going to get points?"

"It's all about making me smile. The bigger the smile . . . the more points," explained Marcus.

"Well, how do I do that? Oh, I know . . . just being me."

"You being you IS worth lots of points," he said.

"Plus, I like grilled cheese and bacon, and other Southern food, and am returning to Texas soon!" I offered.

"Well . . . now you are talking! Huge bonus points have just been awarded," Marcus announced.

"You are going to have to do better than that!" I said. "We haven't even spoken, and you are making snap judgments about how many points I can earn. Shouldn't my slightly Southern accent count for something? If you actually want to hear it AND my copyrighted voice mail, call and leave me a message. I won't pick up," I instructed. "Then you can decide how many points that's worth. And I'll be able to hear what a Californian turned Texan sounds like!"

A few minutes later, my cell phone rang. And then a text from Marcus followed.

"Love your voice. BIG POINTS.

Bet it's even better in person. BIGGER POINTS.

Hopefully, I'll find out one day. HUGE POINTS."

"Let's hope! You could always come meet me at baggage claim the next time I arrive at DFW . . ." I answered.

"And then go back to the airport with you when you head back to NY and stuff myself in the overhead bin," Marcus continued.

"Sounds soooo uncomfortable :)" I replied.

"Well, I won't fit under the seat!" Marcus countered.

I cut to the chase. "How about stepping up to an actual phone conversation at this point? Let's be bold. Call me!"

And he did.

An hour later, when Marcus and I said our goodbyes, we sent texts that crossed over each other.

Mine read: "So enjoyed that not nearly long enough phone call. Love your voice! I will be fascinated to see how it matches my image of you when we meet."

From Marcus: "It was such a pleasure meeting you over the phone, Kate. I really feel we clicked. Absolutely we will stay in touch. . . . that I promise. Travel well this holiday season. Send me random pics when you think about it. :)."

"I'll get back to Texas in February. We will bridge the time 'til then with photos," I pledged.

Over the next month, Marcus and I sent each other "get acquainted" photos every few days. They depicted our moves to new states, our furnishings, New York pictures of snow, or Texas shots in 70-degree weather, and the occasional silly selfie.

With each image he received, Marcus was enthusiastic and responsive in his replies.

"You are adorable!!!

And really beautiful!!

I really love your goofy sense of humor.

You have great taste and incredible style. I just knew that you would.

What's not to like here?!"

I was touched.

"I so appreciate you saying all of this," I answered back. "I've been thinking a lot about what I need in my life. It's about being the best version of myself and finding someone who gets me. I am very impressed that you are doing that so quickly."

"One of my gifts is that I have great discernment," Marcus said.

"You are 100% so far," I acknowledged. "Pray tell, what are your other gifts?"

"You'll have to wait and see," said Marcus.

"Not fair," I said.

"I know I could make you smile," he answered.

I let that text sit for a day, and then I responded.

"I like your confidence!" I came back. "Name one thing."

"Okay, I'll admit: I LOVE to cook and I'm good at it," Marcus answered, quickly.

"You know, I have truly always wanted to cook with someone.

Never did it in my marriage," I said. "But I think it would have been fun."

"Cooking together is sexy. And it IS fun," he answered.

"You are making me hungry!"

"What sounds good?" queried Marcus.

"Everything at the moment :) What are you going to make me? Never mind . . . don't answer that. I'm putting in a request: Salad, your best pasta specialty, and red wine."

"Sounds delicious. Who will fulfill your request?" he asked.

"You—it's your pasta specialty I am ordering, silly!" I laughed.

"I'll make you some good comfort food," Marcus offered. "It goes well with cold snowy weather."

"That's perfect for MY winter. Sure you don't want to be in New York to experience it?" I asked, sending a photo of the Rockefeller Center Christmas tree.

"Thought I was sure . . . now I am not. It's beautiful . . . just like you."

The next day, Marcus initiated the conversation.

"Uh oh . . ." his text began.

"Now, what's rocking your world?" I asked.

"Apparently you!! Caught myself thinking about you again."

"Well, this is getting to be a habit!" I responded.

The next day, I was the one to start the messaging. Our texts were getting closer and closer together.

"My turn . . . happy Friday!" I began.

"Huge bonus points for that!! Good morning, beautiful," answered Marcus.

"Oh, good!!! So, who is winning?" I inquired.

"You just took the lead . . . pressure's on," he announced.

"Hmmmmm . . . can't wait to see your next move!" I came back.

"Well, I am crafty. But I have got it. Name your favorite restaurant in Dallas, and I'll take you there on your next trip back home," promised Marcus. (He always referred to Texas as my home.)

"Just so you know, I had a five-cheese pizza last night. It was pretty great. That's going to be hard to beat." I responded.

"And . . . . it was NY pizza! You, lucky, lucky girl. But answer my question, please madam . . ."

"Well, I haven't had a Texas steak since I've been in NY, so I'll say Del Frisco's."

"Signed, sealed, and delivered. I love that place!" Marcus said. "Just give me the date, and I'll meet you at any Texas location!"

"You mean you would drive anywhere for me? Now that's major points!" I applauded.

"Well, I know there's a Del Frisco's in New York City, but I'll have to get to know you better first! Meanwhile, name the day and time! My only request will be that you wear a white blouse, jeans, and pearls. It's my favorite look, and I bet you could pull it off beautifully with your Texas pedigree," Marcus responded.

"Guess I'll have to bring my boots then."

"Or black heels will do just fine," Marcus replied. "We'll meet for the first time . . . how exciting!"

The next day, our conversation continued. We were both invested in meeting in Texas in February. But that was more than six weeks away.

"My first trip to Texas after New Year's. It's going to be a great new year!" I messaged one morning in early January. "I hope."

"Don't hope! Ask and you shall receive! It's going to be GREAT!" Marcus forecast.

"Can you believe it? I practically know everything there is to know about you already, haha. (What a joke!)" I teased.

"Right?! Well, you get to find out all you want to know in six weeks."

"Everything????? In one visit? Are you going to wear all your clothes and shoes at once?!" I asked.

"Clothes don't define us, cutie," answered Marcus.

"You got that right :) But we have to wear them to make a good first impression," I said.

"Plus, they can accentuate our strengths and sometimes hide our weaknesses," said Marcus.

That night, before he fell asleep, he sent another message:

"I'm doing somersaults over the thought of meeting you, Miss Somerset. And I am resolved to make that happen. No more New Year's resolutions needed!"

The first few weeks of January flew by. Mid-month, Marcus asked for a favorite photo of me to pair with my contact information on his phone. "What photo do you want me to see when your name appears?" he asked.

I texted several choices while sitting at a stoplight in traffic.

"Oh, I like this one," he answered. It was taken on my birthday, smiling at the camera, wearing a black and white leather jacket, and holding a pink balloon. "My eyes seem to gravitate towards your eyes," he went on.

"You mean like in a wax museum?" I inquired. "I can't really ask more. I'm driving."

"Don't text and drive, sweetness. Or you'll get a spanking," admonished Marcus.

"I stopped . . . immediately!" I complied.

The next afternoon, Marcus was in touch again:

"It's the little things, Kate!" he began.

"Like what?" I asked.

"Tomato basil soup.

Grilled cheese.

Grilled cheese and bacon.

NY pizza.

Texas steak.

Watching TV in bed . . . snuggling.

They all could lead to much greater things. . . ." he continued.

"Really?? You mean like foot cramps?" I asked.

"Not like foot cramps, sweetness. But if you like your feet rubbed or any other part of your body . . . I'm your guy."

"I'm filing that under 'useful information Kate needs to know.'"

"To clarify, my hope is to find a real nice girl with values that match mine," Marcus elaborated. "So far . . . Bupkis. Classy girl moved to the Big Apple."

"Well, I am so glad we can at least meet. Compliments of Bumble!" I consoled him. My trip to Texas was less than two weeks away now.

"And" I went on, "I just made our dinner reservation at Del Frisco's. Here's what my Open Table note says:

"I would like a private table for a business conversation, please. Need to impress the guy from Dallas, says the woman from New York. Thank you!"

Marcus had a fast comeback:

"How cute are you? It's like a script from a movie. And I guess that's 'business' ;-) T-minus 8 days . . ."

"Yes, indeed. I am excited. I have dinner with a tall, handsome Californian next week. Happy about that!" I assured him.

The weekend before my trip to Texas, Marcus sent me a thoughtful message. It was obvious he had been pondering what meeting me would be like.

"Do you ever think about whether you might romanticize things before the meet and greet . . . where your expectations are not met after? I'm not trying to stump you with that question. I've done that, and was curious about whether you have too?"

"I absolutely have. And then you spend time mentally trying to adjust once you meet that person to the reality of who they really are," I answered honestly.

"I've learned to set my expectations and meet with an open mind. Unmet expectations are the root of so many problems . . . In families, marriages, work, and life," responded Marcus.

The days before my departure for Texas finally dwindled to one. I packed my white blouse, pearls, and black heels to meet Marcus. I would wear jeans to fly.

The morning of my trip, he sent a message:

"What time is your flight? Are you excited for our rendezvous?"

"Is a child excited for Christmas morning?!" I answered. "How do YOU feel?"

"For me . . . I am interested in finding out if there's chemistry . . . something you can only know by meeting. Then there's whether or not there are sparks in a kiss? If there's chemistry, that leads to a kiss, right?" Marcus continued.

"To give you that answer is to take away the anticipation of discovery. I agree that chemistry is intangible, a mystery. I'm keeping my fingers crossed with you. And my toes too!" I kidded.

"By the way, my flight is early afternoon. I should land in time to get to my hotel and change into the requested dinner attire. I will meet you at the restaurant."

The dinner with Marcus was scheduled for my first night back in Texas. We had figured out it was the only opportunity to meet during my trip. He was flying back to California the next day for a memorial service.

Two hours before my departure, I received a text notification from American Airlines. There was bad weather around New York City, and my flight's departure was delayed by twenty minutes.

Ten minutes later, the delay was updated to forty minutes.

In the taxi on the way to the airport, the forty-minute delay turned into an hour.

Once I got to the airport and checked my luggage, the hour delay had grown to two hours.

I sent Marcus a message.

"My best laid plans," I lamented. "Would you be horribly disappointed if you didn't see the jeans and pearls? There's a two-hour flight delay. If luck is still with me, I will get to Del Frisco's in time to make our reservation. But I will be doing well to ditch the luggage at the restaurant's front door! I have on jeans, but sans the pearls and high heels."

"Let's just get you here in one piece. You'll be beautiful, no matter what!" His words were reassuring.

Our dinner reservation was for 7 PM. My ETA was now 7:18 PM at DFW airport. Then it was another thirty minutes to Dallas and the restaurant. The pilot would have some major in-flight catching up to do!

Once on board, when the doors finally closed and the plane took off, I couldn't sit still. It had been two months since I sent Marcus that first text while taxiing on an American Airlines plane leaving Texas for New York. Now I was headed back to Texas from New York with all our conversation in between and the much-anticipated dinner ahead.

What a fascinating several months since Marcus and I began communicating. The fun of flirting and imagining had been tantalizing for us both.

But would I make it in time for us to actually meet? I didn't want to give up just yet.

As the plane reached the approach to Dallas, the flight attendant came on the intercom. In an uncertain voice, she announced the visibility was so bad we would have to circle indefinitely. The turbulence had moved from Northeast to Southwest. A line of thunderstorms was following me from New York to Texas.

There was no way to notify Marcus of my predicament. All I could do was practice deep yoga breaths each time the plane ricocheted over an air pocket. Physically nauseous from the rough ride and emotionally frustrated with the likely disruption in plans to meet Marcus, it didn't shock me when the flight attendant came back on the intercom.

"Ladies and gentlemen, we are terribly sorry. But we're going to have to divert this flight. We will be circumventing the storms by heading to the closest airport not in the squall's path. We promise to help you find connections and will compensate you for this unexpected outcome of your travel."

That was it. Marcus and I would not meet. At least not this evening.

A full 90 minutes later, my flight bound for DFW landed in Austin, Texas. I texted Marcus while the plane was marooned on the runway, waiting for a gate assignment.

"The weather gods got us," I said, sadly.

"I've been tracking your flight, sweetness. I knew." Marcus answered. "How disappointing!"

He continued. "You know, I've been thinking nonstop about you. About us. I was just sure that once I met you, I was going to fall for you. But you don't live in Texas. And I don't live in New York. So, hard as it is, maybe this outcome is best."

He went on.

"Sure, we could have a long-distance fling. And I know it would be great fun. But then what would we have? Disappointment, heartache, frustration. I don't want to go there. I always want to respect you and not take advantage of our chemistry, which I'm certain we would have. Yes, I would indeed do somersaults over you, Miss Somerset. But ultimately that could be a 'Kate-astrophe' for both of us. My moral code won't let me take advantage of this situation. How fitting that our initial conversation began with you on an airplane, and now this unfortunate conclusion with you on another one.

I'll be flying early in the morning. I'll call you from California to hear your voice. Talk then. Oh, and by the way, I think you are the best thing Bumble ever offered. And these have been the best two months ever. Big hug to you. Have fun in Texas.

Your Marcus."

Would we ever meet? Who knew? The ball was in my court. Until then, the white blouse, pearls, and black heels would stay packed. There was always a possibility.

CAIN the Canine Lover

♪♪ "Hound Dog" ♪♪

Artist: Elvis

In a city of over 8 million people, the surprising coincidence of running into someone you know is a story to recount again and again. And when you bump into a friend who doesn't even live in New York, the surprise creates joy and gives a nod to the notion the world is delightfully small after all.

It was a pleasant Sunday afternoon towards the end of May, and I was walking hurriedly towards a late afternoon lunch about fifteen minutes away. My date and I had texted briefly, but I knew very little about him. Judging from his online profile photo, Cain had an aristocratic face—all angles, with a thin nose and small eyes. His brief bio was definitive in its description.

"I am highly educated and looking for a woman who is the same. I practice law and believe in precision. I can be quite entertaining in conversation and communal activities. Let's meet and discover commonalities."

Given the gorgeous spring weather, I had suggested we meet at an outdoor café, perfect for dining alfresco. And since low humidity and sunshine in tandem can be at a premium in New York City, I knew we'd need a reservation.

"I'll handle it," said Cain, agreeing to my recommended location near Lincoln Center. A small French bistro on the Upper West Side, Luce was the perfect spot to meet someone new. One of several outdoor cafes on the boulevard, it was always pleasantly crowded. And yet there was enough space between tables, so conversations could not easily be overheard.

As I hastily made the half-mile walk from Columbus Circle to

Broadway to join Cain, I wondered what he would be like. I knew he lived in New Jersey and was a lawyer. It appeared he was never married, no kids. Normally that could be a red flag, but it was an afternoon lunch, so there was not much at stake.

"I'm here early," he texted when I was still fifteen minutes away. "I'm wearing a yellow shirt, and tan slacks. If there are two people dressed alike, I'm the better looking one."

"I have on white jeans, a red and taupe top, and a red necklace. And no one is going to be dressed like me. These are Texas clothes, so little competition," I answered with a smile emoji. "I'll be there soon."

"Sitting at a table next to the rail," he replied.

Absorbed in wondering if Cain's abrupt response meant he wasn't thrilled with the restaurant choice, or with me wearing taupe, red, and white, I walked faster. As I rounded the corner in front of the shops at the Time Warner Center, I glanced up at a tall, distinguished man, also walking at a fast clip, and headed straight for me.

"Michael!!" I called out, as we both recognized each other in the same instant. A theater professor from Texas who had collaborated with me in my old life on a music video project, I couldn't believe he was right in front of me.

"Kate!" he exclaimed, as we enthusiastically embraced, forcing the crowds of tourists to split and walk around us.

"What are you doing here?!" I asked, surprised and excited to see him.

"Going to Broadway shows all this week," Michael said. "What are the chances we would run into each other here?! I never even bumped into you in Texas when we were both THERE!

So good to see you in your new home. Where are you hurrying off to on this beautiful Sunday afternoon?"

"Ah," I smiled. "I have a blind date. Frankly, I am not completely sure what I have gotten myself into! You want to come along and be my chaperone?"

Michael laughed. "Are you serious?"

"Completely!" I said while putting the idea into play in my head. "I'll tell my date, Cain, that I ran into an old friend, you offered to walk with me to the restaurant, and that I wanted to introduce you two. Then you can sit down and join us. When it seems logical for you to leave, I'll signal you by saying it was great to see you."

Michael's eyes twinkled. "I don't think I've ever been asked to be the third wheel on a blind date. But it sounds like fun! If you're game, I'm in."

Walking side by side, Michael and I caught up on my new life in New York and his Broadway plans for the rest of the week in the City.

"You know I am going to want an update about this date when it's over," he said.

"Oh, don't worry," I laughed. "My chaperones are always the first to know!"

When Michael and I arrived at the restaurant, I spotted Cain before he saw me. Seated facing us, he was staring at his watch and tapping his foot. "This oughta be fun," I whispered conspiratorially under my breath to Michael. "Here we go!"

When Cain stood up to greet us, Michael towered over him. Not completely sure if I also wasn't taller, we briefly shook hands. I explained who Michael was.

"He won't be staying for lunch," I reassured. "He just wants to say hello."

"I see," said Cain.

"Michael can give you an objective third-party perspective on Kate Somerset that will take you hours to get on your own," I laughed.

"I'm a quick study," Cain countered.

"I won't stay long," said Michael. He and I pulled out chairs to face opposite Cain. After we sat, Michael directed his attention to Cain. "Tell me about yourself," he said in a friendly, but protective way.

"I am a successful attorney," Cain began, "retired now, and still proud of the fact that I could discover loopholes in tax laws where no one else could. I have a head for math."

And with that, he launched into an explanation of a complicated tax case. Twenty minutes passed before a waiter came over to ask what we might like to drink.

"I have my water," he said. "What would you two like?"

When the waiter brought an iced tea for me and a coffee for Michael, Cain still had not finished his story about the years-long tax case. As a bread basket was placed on the table, he dismissively waved his hand towards it.

"I am not having any," he said. "I pride myself on not eating between meals. But feel free . . ."

With a quick smile and a wink, Michael poured olive oil onto my bread plate and passed the overflowing basket of crusty bread to me. "You must be famished," he said, "since you told me you hadn't eaten breakfast. And it's past lunchtime now."

Smiling at Michael, I replied. "How kind of you! Please have some too!"

A brief arch of Cain's eyebrows registered his discontent that both Michael and I were tearing off big chunks of hot bread and dipping them into olive oil as he talked. Still, he continued.

Michael and I had devoured all the bread when the topic switched from Cain's legal knowledge to family. Still, no mention of the promised late lunch, and no request for the menu.

"So, do you have children?" I asked.

"No," he said. "I've never found anyone I wanted to be married to. But I do have a beautiful puppy named Daisy, who is my girl. Want to see a picture?" he asked, whipping out his phone.

When he proudly handed it over, I saw that Cain had created separate photo albums titled by Daisy's activities. Samples included:

Daisy Running
Daisy Jumping
Daisy Sitting
Daisy Rolling Over
Daisy Getting a Treat
Daisy Sleeping
Daisy Stretching
Daisy Barking (a five-minute video)

Every Daisy action was captured close up, with multiple angles, and shown off to Michael and me with uncontained, breathless pride.

"That's my girl!" he gushed.

"That's my girl!" he repeated, beaming.

I could feel Michael shift in his chair next to me, but I dared not look at him for fear of convulsing into an uncontrollable fit of laughter. When I had regained a sense of internal composure, I leaned over to Michael and gave him a side hug.

"You are so great to have spent so much of your afternoon with me," I offered, not mentioning Cain. "I really hope we can see each other again soon."

"Wouldn't have missed it for the world!" said Michael in his best actor's voice.

"Anything I can share with you about our wonderful Kate here?" Michael asked.

"No, thank you," Cain said, sniffing the air. "I prefer to do my own investigations. I am a good judge of character."

"Well, then, I'll be on my way." While Cain remained seated, I stood up to receive Michael's hug and whispered message in my ear: "I am a good judge of character too!"

I watched Michael walk down the sidewalk back in the direction of Lincoln Center. Once he was out of view, I turned around and sat down. Immediately, Cain was up and out of his chair, his short, slim body leaning over me. Startled, I looked up into his small face.

Without warning, he kissed me on the lips, stood up satisfied, and pronounced:

"I just had to do that! You are a beautiful creature."

In that moment, I knew with certainty I was taller than Cain. Standing up, he looked even skinnier than he had sitting down. Seeing his thin physique, I wondered about his discipline of not eating between meals. This was to be a lunch date, and it was already 3:00 PM.

"Are you hungry?" I asked.

"Oh, no!" he said. "I'll need to go home soon to let Daisy out. And then I'll eat when she eats. It's our routine."

"In fact, the poor girl is probably getting anxious," he went on. "Let's talk for a bit more and make plans for the next time I'll see you. Then let's go, and I'll drive you to wherever you are headed. I'd like you to see my car."

"If it's not out of your way, I'd be happy for you to drop me at the train station."

"Done," he said.

Cain arched his eyebrows when the check came and let out a loud sigh. All we had consumed was the bread basket, an iced tea and a coffee. I mentally calculated that the tab couldn't have been more than $20, even by Manhattan standards.

"Can I help?' I asked. "No," he said, "I am just always amazed how these places try to stiff you."

We walked out of the restaurant and onto the sidewalk, as Cain attempted to put his short arm around me.

"We're going to be good together. Do you like dogs? It may take some time because Daisy is a one-owner dog, but I predict she will eventually like you."

"Well, I always want to gamble on the right side of the equation," I said.

"Exactly. That's why I don't go into casinos."

Cain's car was parked a few blocks away in a garage. When the attendant delivered the dark blue BMW to the pay booth, Cain walked around the car three times to check for any scratches, dents, or other insults to his vehicle.

"How much is that again?" he asked when told the parking fee. "Wow, good thing it's a Sunday. I wouldn't want to pay your weekday rates."

On the drive to the train station, he kept up the chatter. "So, what's your political persuasion? I have worked with state and local officials for years. I know the truth. I think the media blows everything out of proportion these days."

Before I could answer, the train station loomed ahead. "Oh, here we are," I said. "I need to jump out at this corner." As I reached for the door handle with my right hand, Cain grabbed my other hand and slammed on the brakes.

"I'll be back in the City on Tuesday to have my BMW serviced," he announced, as irritated drivers behind us blared their horns. "Have an early dinner while I wait for the car? Of course, I'll have to get back to let Daisy out."

"Sure," I said, sticking to my 'always give the guy a second chance' rule. "See you then."

Back at home, I texted Cain:

"Thank you so much for this afternoon. It was interesting to hear about your work. Hope your drive was easy, and that all was well with Daisy."

He answered back in seconds:

"Wow. I was really getting worried about Daisy, but she was OK. Great day."

Later that evening, Michael sent me a message:

"How did the rest of the time go with Cain?"

"He asked me out again for Tuesday. What did you think of him?" I hedged the bet before giving my own opinion.

"I didn't get a sense of his ability to engage," Michael said. "I always think in terms of how a person would handle himself socially—with my professional contacts, as well as my close friends, and especially when we are on opposite sides of a room. As far as seeing him again, keep going! On the hard-core side of things, it's a numbers game, just like auditions. The more you show up for, the better!"

And in that spirit, on Tuesday, I met Cain for a very early dinner. Again, I picked, choosing a small restaurant close to the auto garage where his car was being worked on.

It was 5:30 PM when we met, and the restaurant was empty except for one other table of two men, loudly negotiating the finer points of an entertainment deal. We were seated right next to them, so it was impossible not to overhear snippets of their conversation.

I was intrigued.

Cain was not.

When I slipped away to the lady's room, I saw him motion for the waiter. On returning, Cain was sitting at another table far away from the pair of men. Puzzled, I sat down at the new spot and asked:

"So, how'd you get us moved?"

"Simple," he said. "I told the waiter that my girlfriend was very offended by the loud talking of those gentlemen. I went on to say that I insisted we have a new table, as I wanted to be sensitive to your needs."

Shocked that he would set me up to be the complainant AND refer to me as his girlfriend, I looked at Cain in blank disbelief. He appeared not to notice at all and began another story about one of his many legal successes. Even though they were across the room, the entertainment duo's topics were what I strained to hear as Cain talked on.

He ordered a salad at which he halfheartedly picked, so he had more time to talk about his bar victories and his clever maneuverings to secure the outcomes he wanted. I sipped a bowl of soup and indulged (again) on the bread.

"So, tell me about the dogs you've had," he said, finally changing the subject. "My Daisy is so smart I wonder if you've ever had a puppy that could do what she can do. For example, I am potty training her now. When I got home yesterday, she was very, very happy to see me. And no accidents. So, I rewarded her with a treat. A pig's ear. I was surprised to find them in the pet section. I bought them, and she loved them."

"She has you totally wrapped around her paws," I said.

"Yes, but so did Spanky." (I didn't ask!) "It's worth it!" he went on.

Our dinner didn't last much longer since the garage was closing at 7 PM, and Cain had to retrieve his car.

"I'll just call a taxi to get to my train," I said, dashing out the restaurant's front door.

"I had a terrific time," he hollered after me. "You're such a great conversationalist!"

On this night, before I could write a follow-up text, Cain sent his:

"My car was ready, and they didn't charge me too much. I really enjoyed this evening. The first moment I saw you on Sunday, I knew I would be comfortable with you. I don't know why that happened, but it did. By the way, do you know where the expression 'sleep tight' comes from?"

"Gosh, I'm scared to ask."

"Good. I'll tell you when I see you again. Don't cheat and look it up. In the meantime, sleep tight and sweet dreams."

"You should never tell a woman you want her not to do something . . . because she might just go do it," I answered.

"So that's why Daisy keeps jumping on me when I tell her to get down," Cain replied.

"And how does Daisy figure into this again?" I questioned.

"She's a woman that does the opposite of what I say."

"Good for her!" I fired back.

"I think she secretly likes me. Do you?" Cain asked.

"Do I think she secretly likes you? I doubt it's a secret," I answered, subverting his question's likely intent.

"You're right. She's very sweet. I enjoy your company and am looking forward to seeing you again. And you are very beautiful, smart, and sweet."

Over the next month, Cain asked me out every week, usually by email. Between travel and other work obligations, I was either unavailable or not inclined to go.

"I got your emails. Sounds like you're working very hard. I wish there was something I could do to make it easier for you," he sounded slightly concerned.

"Buy me a helicopter. With the pilot." I teased.

"I'll start my flying lessons tomorrow. If I were your pilot, I'd notice what you were wearing. Then I'd put the copter on autopilot." Cain stepped it up.

"You do love adventure, don't you? Or something." I answered.

"Absolutely. I think we would enjoy each other's company and have a lot of fun. And maybe Daisy would like to come along."

More weeks passed and Cain kept the texts coming.

"Just thinking of you. Daisy and I hope you are having a good week."

"Hope you are doing well and not working quite so hard."

"Looking forward to seeing you for more great talks."

"I am sitting with Daisy. I don't think she's feeling well. Just got up to check on her and happy to call you. Otherwise, another time. Sweet dreams."

"Daisy is much better. Up and about with her toys, but still not much appetite. I'll keep a close eye, but I'm relieved. Please don't be at all concerned about me. You have enough to be concerned about with your work. I'll be here. Until next time, sleep tight and sweet dreams."

I acknowledged each message with brief ones of my own. To the last one I said:

"So glad Daisy is better. Thank you for being so kind about my schedule. Have a good month."

"Have fun and stay away from strange men!" Cain advised.

"Not counting you?!" I teased.

"No, I am not strange. You are fun, and I am so looking forward to seeing you again."

The next week, a photo of Daisy popped onto my phone screen accompanied by this text:

"Today she pooped in my house and peed in my car, but I still love her. Is there something wrong with me or is that just a good sign for any girl I fall in love with?"

"I think you need to set better boundaries with women," I answered.

"Just kidding," Cain quickly came back. "She's only six months old. She'll be fine."

At the beginning of July, he sent a photo of Daisy running along a manicured, leafy outdoor path in a residential area.

"Hi. Hope you're having a good day. Thought I'd show you what the landscaping looks like just outside my door. That's Daisy racing back to me. I don't know where you are, but hope you have a great 4th."

I was traveling abroad and didn't respond promptly. When I returned from the trip, I called Cain to tell him it was time he should move on. It was a cordial conversation. He acknowledged that our lives did not sync up and wished me well.

A month later, as if we had never had that talk, Cain sent an out of the blue message:

"It was so funny. We were at a nature preserve. There weren't any people around, so I let Daisy off her leash, and she was running everywhere, sniffing and exploring. Then she saw the ducks sitting near the water. She took off like a rocket after them. They flew off but, to my amazement, she launched herself into the air after them. It was actually a beautifully perfect and very long leap. She would've gotten a ten in the Olympics. However, it took me a very long struggle with her in the bathtub to get all of the mud out of her fur.

Anyway, I'm sorry you don't want to continue. I was looking forward to seeing you again. You're very beautiful, smart and personable and I'm sure you'll have an easy time finding someone. Just be a little circumspect. A successful career will bring you satisfaction and money, but at the end of the day, it's no substitute for happiness. I made that mistake once.

Best of luck, Cain."

I did my best to construct a gracious response:

"Daisy sounds like a full-time joy! Thanks for the words of advice. I started thinking this morning that I began my dating adventure two months and one week ago. It was wonderful to meet you in literally the first of those weeks. At this moment, what I do know is that I cannot be in a serious relationship. I'm learning a lot about myself in this process."

"Since you just started your life in New York, I agree," said Cain. "You need to establish yourself, and that should be the priority, but it might be wise to set a date certain down the road maybe six months or a year to reassess priorities. It's so easy to get lost in a career.

By the way, I think I might've found my girl. I met her, in all places at the BMW service department where we both were having our cars serviced. It's early, but it's promising.

And so, Kate, I believe in life you never go back, and that means you and I are not going to be together. However, you're one of the rare people I've met who I enjoy talking with and whose opinions I respect.

From time to time, people who know me call for advice about all kinds of situations and I'm always happy to help. I seem to have an intuitive ability to understand problems involving human conflicts and to see the proper strategy to deal with them. (Even if it's just two guys talking too loud at dinner. Remember that?)

So, if you ever need advice or would just like to talk about an issue, I would be happy to help or just listen. I've been doing this since I was a teenager and never revealed a confidence."

"That's such a generous offer," I thanked him. "I'll stay in touch."

And several months later I did, sending a quick text greeting.

"Nice to hear from you," he answered. "Hope everything is going well for you and that you have a wonderful autumn. Daisy is fine. She's nine months old now and getting better behaved . . . Well, for the most part. It's funny, but I was just thinking about you yesterday and wondering how you were doing."

"And I have been wondering about you," I replied. "Did the girlfriend from the car dealership work out?"

"Still seeing her but beginning to have some doubts. We'll see. It could just be me," Cain said. "Yes. Maybe it's just me, but I don't think a conversation about developing a relationship should include specifications for a house in New Jersey with a pool and a winter place in Florida. I think I'll move to Louisiana and find a nice girl who would be tickled pink to have her own little place right on the bayou. With a porch and all. We could spend our days fishing with her cousins and our nights drinking shine and making love to the sound of the frogs croaking."

"I am not a fan of Louisiana humidity," I answered. "But I am sure there are lovely people there. And I am laughing about your demanding girlfriend!"

"It's just so frustrating trying to find someone," Cain fussed. "The thing that bothers me is how could someone who is with me not understand that she could have anything she wants? Why feel you have to ask for it? Just joking about Louisiana. If I tied up with a girl named Daisy Mae, it would just confuse Daisy. That's part of what attracted me to you. You didn't need anything from me—you're independent, confident, and talented. So, any relationship we had would have been without any other motive. Just too bad it couldn't have worked."

"I appreciate the compliments very much," I replied. "Here's to a great Sunday for you and Daisy!"

A month later, a lightning bolt message landed from Cain that wasn't about Daisy.

"I can't believe all the women making harassment allegations against so many men . . . Even Bush 41 who is very, very old. What do you make of all this? You've been in the business world and you're very attractive. Has this happened to you? I was in a power position for years, but no woman has come forward saying that I groped her. I'm beginning to feel I missed out. But really, what about all these allegations? Charlie Rose is being accused. This is getting funny. Your take?"

I had to respond. I waited several hours first and then chose my words carefully.

"I really don't take any of this lightly. You are not a female. Happens all the time."

"You're right," Cain admitted. "But now it's becoming real to even guys. I had no idea. Because I wouldn't do it, I had no real idea how bad it was. Or how common. Sorry if I took it lightly."

"It's SO commonplace," I answered. "I admire the women who are speaking out. They are demonstrating real courage."

"Why did they wait so long?" Cain argued. "This bothers me. I pay attention to what's going on, but when the media and the women don't take it seriously, why would I know to?"

"The women DO take it seriously. If you were a victim, trust me that you would never forget. They just don't want to be crucified, so they wait for safety in numbers. This is a watershed moment to see that women can stand together and speak out," I emphasized.

"Matt Lauer, Congressman Conyers, Garrison Keillor, President Bush, President Clinton, wow it doesn't stop. This is bizarre, but I guess women were always aware. Now I'm retired, but with every news article, I'm thinking there are a lot of high-paying opportunities for guys who have not molested any women. Let me know when someone in your company gets fired. Maybe I could get that job. It would have to pay a lot and be pet-friendly. Daisy is a female. Let me know."

I didn't respond. And that was my last exchange with Cain.

At Christmas, I sent "chaperone" Michael a holiday greeting.

"It was so terrific to see you this summer in New York. Thank you for going with me on the date with Cain. In every interaction he and I had, I applied the 'opposite side of the room' test.

I won't say more except that your advice put my brief time with him into the perfect context. Too bad you can't come with me on ALL my dates!!"

Michael's response made me smile.

"I have to admit I enjoyed it. And besides, I loved telling my friends about our 'date'. Most of them thought I was making it up. And I got great stories about you that day that I had never heard. Any time."

"Well, you are hired!!" I answered.

"There you go—my New Yorker friends would be proud. In the meantime, I expect progress reports from you."

"You wouldn't believe it if I told you," I said truthfully. "I couldn't make these stories up."

SAUL the Sailor

♫ Rock the Boat ♫

Artist: The Hues Corporation

It was the first week in June and my second full week of dating. I was happily surprised my dance card was full every night. And I was especially looking forward to dinner at the Oyster Bar in Grand Central on Thursday night. The lawyer, who sounded both smart and sassy on our phone call, likely was the most promising of the seven planned dates.

Early Thursday morning, I heard from a new online match. When Saul asked to get together that same day, I began the mental calculation. The only time I had open was late afternoon. Would I have time to squeeze in another date before a work meeting at 6:00 PM and my Oyster Bar dinner date at 7:00 PM?

"You appear to be a distinguished lady, possessed of wisdom and wit," Saul messaged me on the Our Time dating app. "Where do you live? The Upper East Side? If so, might you be interested in a quick, light lunch in early afternoon?"

"Thanks so much for the invitation," I answered. "I am sitting on a train headed into Manhattan and won't arrive in time for lunch. But where might you be in the late afternoon? I am going to Grand Central Terminal at the end of the day for a meeting and then a dinner at the Oyster Bar."

"Ah, that's a respectable spot, if not a bit touristy," Saul opined. "I'll also be at GC later too. I am headed to a dinner in CT. NY factoid: Grand Central had the same architect as the New York Yacht Club which was built about ten years earlier."

"Thank you for that historical reference," I responded. "Grand

Central is a beautiful building. I have not been to the New York Yacht Club. What time are you in Grand Central today? Maybe we can wave at each other. The 3D version of me is much more interesting than the online one!"

"Nice. Let's comm later to see if we can sync," Saul answered.

I was looking forward to being in Grand Central. The famous train terminal, first opened to the public in 1913, is a center of commerce. With 60 shops, 35 restaurants, and train tracks on two levels, the building is a beehive of activity, day and night.

Passengers running down escalators and marble steps to catch trains, and tourists gaping at the enormous chandeliers, soaring ceilings, and giant American flag are common sights. Friends meeting by the famous clock at the circular information desk find the perfect backdrop for countless selfies. Grand Central Terminal is a destination on its own, even if you never buy a ticket or ride a train. Experiencing the hustle and bustle is a New York City tradition.

For commuters, Grand Central houses Metro-North Railroad, which carries thousands of passengers a day to stops north of New York City. Trains come and go at all hours, to towns in Westchester County and cities in Connecticut. Subways tracks underneath the massive building connect trains to all parts of Manhattan and other boroughs.

The ambiance of Grand Central is old-world romantic. How many first meetings, planned or unplanned, happen at Grand Central? I wondered. And in my case, it was looking like there would be two in one day. Surely not a record, but it still felt exciting to me!

"I am not likely to make it to GC by 4:30 PM," Saul had texted earlier. "What time will you be leaving the building?"

"I have a meeting across the street at Cipriani at 6:00 PM to preview an event space. But I'll come back to Grand Central after," I replied, without feeling compelled to reveal that the Oyster Bar meeting was a date. "Anytime between 4:30 and 6:00 would be open for me."

"Okay, I will text or call when I get there," Saul replied. "I have to tell you that I never do this . . . meet someone that I haven't fully investigated. But your profile was so strong, I am making an exception."

Without commenting on Saul's revelation, I gave him details about how to find me.

"I'll be sitting at Irving Roasters downstairs by track 107," I explained. "I am wearing a navy suit, a pink necklace, and pink lipstick. Take a look, and if you don't like what you see, you can keep moving."

"You'll recognize me," Saul answered back. "I look like a male version of a bag-lady with everything I am carrying."

Late in the afternoon, as I found my seat across from track 107, I got a text update:

"Next stop on the subway, GC," Saul reported. "I wasn't planning on taking the subway. Of course, you'd be worth the Uber ride, but the pickup line was too long."

The community tables on the lower level of Grand Central were crowded and almost completely occupied during rush hour. I was lucky to have snagged a seat on a long wooden bench with a table in front. I staked the chair opposite me with my shoulder bag for Saul.

Now, as ready as I would ever be, I texted him.

"Come find me. I have a water bottle in my hand, and my *Wall Street Journal* is on the table in front of me. I am consumed with writing emails, so I might not be aware when you arrive. Like you, I have little information about you, starting with what you look like. Your profile picture showed you looking down. I want to see your face!"

Minutes later, the deep resonance of a "radio announcer" voice startled me. The booming sound was coming from a man whose physical height was most surely less than mine.

"Hello, Kate," he said mellifluously. "I circled to look at you three times, each angle more compelling than the last. May I sit down?"

Indeed small in stature, but powerful in presence, Saul had cropped white hair and wore distinguished wire-rimmed glasses. His dark suit was professional and commanding, and he held himself with a disciplined posture.

His blue eyes bore into mine. He didn't look away, even as he set his overflowing canvas bag on the floor and pulled out the chair. What did that look mean? Was he curious or intrigued?

He smiled. Immediately I saw the gap between his two front teeth. David Letterman-like, it was both noticeable and hard to ignore. I focused on his eyes.

Saul began with questions. Our conversation was an audition.

> "Where did you go to school?
> Where do you live?
> How did you get to New York?
> Do you know anyone in the fine gems business (his work)?
> How many children do you have?
> Do you want to get married again?"

At one point, Saul got up and retrieved a china coffee cup from Irving Roasters, asking for ice water. "I don't consume coffee, tea, or soft drinks," he said when he returned to the table. "This and cold milk are my drinks of choice. Occasionally, I will have a glass of champagne or an aperitif. I see you have your bottle of water. I like that you make healthy choices."

As he gulped his water, Saul's interrogation continued: "Do you like sailing? I work hard eight months of the year, so I can engage in my real love . . . sailing. I have a large boat I keep in Europe. I sailed it there single-handed 17 years ago. Every summer I go back and host guests on the boat until mid-September. In fact, I leave next week. It's a pity we met so late. You could always come to Sweden. But first I would have to see you as many times as possible before I go. What are you doing this week?"

My head reeling, I turned the questions back to Saul before answering:

> "Tell me about your boat.
> Does it have a name?
> How many does it sleep?
> Where do you sail?
> Who sails with you?
> Will you ever bring the boat back to the States?"

"My boat is called 'Stop Watch' since I am in the jewelry business," Saul answered. "I never want to 'stop watching' the beauty I see from her deck. I have friends of forty years who come aboard each summer. And I invite other guests, both from Europe and the United States. I don't have a staff. I do it all—cook, maintain the boat, and captain. I give my guests duties when they come aboard. Someday I may bring the boat back. But no matter where it is, I want to find someone to share it with, who enjoys it as much as I do.

I'm hosting a clambake tomorrow and Saturday at my home for people from all over the world who have been on my boat. It's a pity that I couldn't have asked you, but I already have a date . . . some model I don't even know. Frankly, she's rather vacant and insufferable. But I predict survival."

An hour had passed. Saul glanced at his watch. "My train will be here shortly. I must go. But before I do, I must tell you that you check all the boxes. I could take you anywhere," he said, almost as if he was speaking to himself. "So, are you available on Sunday night? I normally don't do this, but I would invite you to my home. I'll make an exception in this case, as I think it would be instructive for you to see how I live."

"Thank you. I can let you know tomorrow. I am in Philadelphia on Saturday and back for a work event in Larchmont, New York, on Sunday afternoon."

By this time, we were standing up. I was right. My gaze crested the top of Saul's head.

Flashing another tooth-gapped smile at the base of the stairs, Saul made his exit. "I shall await your answer with great anticipation," he called out in his sonorous voice.

That evening, Saul sent me a message:

"I knew—well, let's say I was almost certain—with our exchanges and your profile that you'd be fine. You weren't just fine; you were great."

"Thanks so much, Saul. Are you glad that you broke your rules? You hadn't learned my last name, you hadn't spoken to me on the phone, and you most certainly had not been able to google me."

"Very glad," he replied. "And you broke those rules too, so I hope you are as pleased as I am with your good judgment."

"Thanks again for today," I answered.

"You're very welcome. I thank you. It's kind of funny, actually: first 'date' in the basement of GC where we drank water. Yours was in a bottle. Might have cost you something. Mine was free."

"Do you eat anything unhealthy?" I asked.

"Yes, I shouldn't, but I do eat Pommes Frites—if made the French bistro-style, thin. And I've even eaten chocolate chip cookies twice. Only to be consumed with milk. Enough about food. It's now time to turn our brains completely off. So good night. Pleasant dreams."

The next day, I let Saul know that my Sunday afternoon work event would end in time for me to meet him in the evening.

"I am a night owl, so the start time doesn't matter to me. It takes me a long time to settle down in the evening," I explained.

"Usually takes me about 1.5 seconds to fall asleep," Saul responded. "You can train yourself, and you should. What time do you usually get up? This time of year, for me with the early light, it's around 5:30 AM. I feel lazy otherwise."

"I won't keep you out late then," I promised. "What do you have in mind?"

"Something simple. There will likely be leftovers from my party. Do you like lemonade? If not, someone gave me a bottle of champagne. I'll make an exception and drink it with you. And of course, I have milk.

Must go now . . . back to mix a couple of punches for tmrw and to rejoin house guests—very close friends. I have known one of them since first grade. She married a great friend of mine since eighth grade. The others are more recent, like 30-plus years. Yours, Saul."

Two nights later, I pulled up in front of Saul's large home. Driving to the affluent neighborhood on the peninsula of the Long Island Sound had been breathtaking at sunset. In between the footprints of the expensive homes on expansive lots, I marveled at the glimpses of orange-hued light from the setting sun dancing on the water.

Entering Saul's property from the street, I turned down the long gravel driveway and circled to pull up in front of the door. The house's architecture resembled a magnified Cape Cod, with an L-shaped front, decorative shutters, and a pitched, gabled roof. The lawn to the side of the house sloped to the water. The view was majestic.

Saul's foreign car was parked in front with the vanity license plate 'Stop Watch' visible as I pulled in behind.

Appearing outside his front glass storm door, Saul stood even smaller than at our first meeting. Gone were the suit and wingtip shoes. A solid-colored navy single-pocket T-shirt, khaki slacks, and black tennis shoes replaced the work attire. He seemed older and less imposing.

"Come in, honey," he said as if he had known me for years. "I've been waiting for you."

There were no remaining signs of the party. The house looked unlived in and dark. The two connecting living rooms off the entry appeared as if they were never used. Sheets covered the furniture (surely, they had been removed for the party!) and the heavy drapes were closed.

Saul led me back to the kitchen, the ceiling lit with fluorescent neon strips. The light was harsh compared to the dimly lit small Venetian glass chandelier hanging in the entry.

On the counter by the sink, Saul had set out two dinner plates. Each had a bed of lettuce and two slices of tomatoes on top.

"How about a little crabmeat left over from my weekend? The crackers are in there," he said, gesturing to a cabinet across the room. "Why don't you look in the fridge to see what kind of salad dressing I have?"

As I rifled through half-eaten boxes of saltine crackers and Wheat Thins, my appetite decreased with each discovery. The cracker collection looked like it had been undisturbed for a long time.

"I don't require anything crunchy with MY salad," Saul announced. "Hope you find what you are looking for. My houseboy is supposed to keep inventory and let me know when I run out of something."

The bottled salad dressing selection in the fridge was equally meager. After looking through the offerings, I declared I didn't need dressing.

"That's my girl. I like my crabmeat straight out of the tub," he said, pulling out a half-filled grocery store plastic container, and spooning chunks of meat on top of the tomatoes. "It's better for you that way," he went on, as he got out a carton of milk and poured himself a tall glass.

"I even got you some chocolate chip cookies," he said proudly, as he pointed toward a grocery-bought package of Keebler's. "They are my grandson's favorite!"

A step down from the kitchen, the eat-in sunroom revealed damage that Hurricane Sandy wreaked five years earlier. Water had seeped into the house and warped the floor, which had not been repaired. Large foam alphabet puzzle pieces were laid out to cover the exposed concrete.

We ate our dinner at the sunroom's simple wooden table. Saul gulped his cold milk, licking his lips with every swallow, and quickly got himself a refill. He offered me drinking water out of the tap, served in a large plastic cup from a local pizza restaurant.

Over the meal, Saul regaled me with stories of sailing.

"The more I think about it, the more you must come. I will send you the schedule of my entire summer and you pick the time," he said. "You can sleep in the V-berth in front of the boat. And if I am lucky, so can I!"

After dinner, he opened the champagne—the gift from his friends—and proposed a toast to the idea of my travel to Sweden. The champagne flutes, pulled from the back of a kitchen cupboard, reminded me of my grandmother's juice glasses from five decades before.

After the toast, Saul carried the champagne bottle and glasses into the darkened dining room where paintings hung covered by brown bath towels (to keep the sunlight off, he explained). He pulled two straight-back wooden dining room chairs in front of the window which looked out onto the jet-black waters of Long Island Sound. Through the darkness, I glimpsed the faint edge of the Manhattan skyline in the distance.

When the champagne bottle was drained, Saul led me back to the kitchen and reached for me next to the dishwasher where I had earlier loaded our dinner plates.

"Promise me you'll come to Sweden," he said in his deep voice, as he leaned in towards me.

Then rocking back on his heels with a tentative hand on my back, he suddenly lurched forward as he planted his lips on mine. Besides tasting the smell of crabmeat on his breath, I was acutely aware of his two front teeth crashing into mine. Enamel on enamel. The clinking sound made me grateful I never wore braces or ever kissed anyone who did.

I pulled back.

"Thank you for a lovely evening," I said. "I really must be going. I have a long drive."

He led me to the door and opened it to a driving rainstorm. The giant drops hit the gravel driveway like pellets cascading from the sky. Refusing the offer of an umbrella, I raced to my car and jumped in.

Without the benefit of any landscape lighting to illuminate the long gravel driveway, I started backing up, hoping for the best. "Stop! Stop! Not THAT way," Saul yelled. Even with my windows up, I could hear his voice.

Out of one eye, I could see him jumping up and down in front of my car. My other eye was staring straight at foliage scraping my side-view mirror. In that split second, I realized I was not on the driveway, but headed straight through the grass into a thicket of flowering trees.

Self-correcting, I shifted my steering wheel to get back on course. Waving and motioning an apology through the windshield wipers, I drove away. It didn't help that my one glass of champagne had given me a headache and that the rain was coming down in sheets.

To his credit, Saul checked on me several times on my hour and a half drive home.

"You know I made an exception to date someone who lives so far away. But you seem like you can handle yourself. I predict survival," he said in one of his calls.

When I got home, I sent him a text of thanks.

"Lovely evening. Thanks for sending me home with the package of Keebler's cookies. I ate them in the car. That was generous."

Saul replied. "Merci. Toi Aussi. (From the little French I know. I've tried my whole life—tutors, etc. Made sure my kids went to school there, albeit briefly, and worked there.) Suffit, le temps de dormir. Beaux reves."

"You are outdoing yourself. Merci!" I answered.

Saul was traveling the next week to Sweden. Before he left, he invited me for dinner and a tour of the New York Yacht Club. Learning about sailing through his eyes and vast experience was enlightening. I was treated to a private tour of the model room with its 1230 models of yachts and ships. Saul waxed eloquent about the most famous sailing competitions, how racing boats are made, and the history of the iconic building and its membership-only Club.

Pulling me behind one of the stunning glass cases which displayed an America's Cup trophy, Saul kissed me and sighed. "You ask great questions," he said. "I am glad to have such an appreciative audience."

Our dinner at the Club was the sendoff for Saul's four months at sea. When I stepped into a cab at the end of our evening, I wondered if I would hear from him again soon.

But no sooner than he arrived across the sea, Saul began sending daily missives on an encrypted messaging app.

"Thinking of you yesterday, today, and tomorrow.

Your voicemail seems tailored just for me. Extremely nice. With humor. It's very welcoming. I don't even remember mine. Possibly a little brusque or the standard Apple answer.

The last voicemail I left you when I was stateside asked how I should address you: Kate Somerset? Katie? Kate sweetness?

Dearest Kate-for-now, please come to Sweden. You say you can't sleep on a plane. I am six hours away. Your eyes will look great, even if bleary. I've looked hard at them. Which is rare for me. I cannot tell you the color of anyone's eyes, even in my family, but for some inexplicable reason I looked at your eyes with real intensity, which struck me at that moment, the fact of looking so hard."

After Saul's first week in Sweden, we began more serious negotiations about my coming to visit. It was an open invitation. He offered me any time frame I wished . . . a week, two, or more in any of the months he would be there.

"I will pay to get you here," he went on. "I am happy to buy you an economy ticket. You will fly through the night and arrive in time for us to start sharp in the morning."

"Thank you," I said. "But honestly, I don't sleep well on airplanes without reclining."

"You'll be able to sleep sitting up. Remember, you can teach yourself. Or upgrade the ticket on your own if you wish. I like independent women," Saul went on. "It would be good to know that you can pay the difference."

"My sleeping well on a plane would make for an interesting midsummer night's dream," I countered.

"Made me chuckle out loud. Very clever," Saul rejoined.

And again, he repeated: "I made an exception to date you because you didn't go to an Ivy League school. But it looks like it was another good decision on my part."

Now I had to make my own decision: go or not go to Sweden to sail with a man I had seen only a few times in just under a week. Talked into saying yes by friends and my sister, I decided the adventure was worth the risk. I'd probably never get an authentic sailing experience like the one Saul offered, even if it might mean for some awkward moments.

"I do feel the need to clarify the arrangements," I said, upon accepting. "You know, we've only known each other for a week. Although I really look forward to coming to see you in Sweden for a few days, you're going to be gone all summer. I am newly off the divorce boat and just starting to date. What are your expectations for this visit?"

"Honey, I predict survival. I'm sure once you get here, you will be thoroughly enchanted. And all my friends will love to meet the woman of my dreams," he responded.

When I landed in Sweden in early morning, exhausted by going 36 hours with no sleep, I still had to take two more forms of transportation to get to Saul. First a long car trip, and then a ferry ride would finally get me to Marstrand, the seaport city where Saul's boat was to be docked.

At the end of that journey, deposited at the gates of the ferry, I stood alone in a strange land with one too many heavy suitcases. There was no transportation in sight. I asked a local where the hotel was. He pointed to the top of the hill up a steep cobblestone path. Cursing myself for overpacking, I pulled one suitcase and pushed the other, my shoulder bag slipping from my arm, and my feet swollen and stuck in my shoes from the long international flight.

But when I got to the charming small hotel, my luck changed. Saul texted that headwinds were delaying his boat and the others he was leading. They could not sail to Marstrand from the town where they were, but would arrive the next day. I had the night to myself!

But my time to recover was short-lived.

The next morning at 8 AM, Saul had gained entrance to the hotel room while I was still sleeping. Groggy from the time change, I opened one eye to see him standing at the edge of the bed. Clutching the covers, I lurched into a seated position.

"It's great to see you, honey," he said, in his booming voice. "But get dressed right now. We have to go tour the fort. Everybody is waiting for you."

And he wasn't kidding. As the leader of a fleet of nineteen sailboats on a western archipelago cruise of Sweden, Saul had been talking nonstop about my arrival with his fellow sixty travelers. When I arrived at the fort, his sailing companions were practically lined up to introduce themselves to me.

"It's SO great to meet you."

"Saul's been dying for you to arrive."

"We are really glad you two have found each other."

"You're going to be very happy together."

"Finally! Saul has met a good one! He should not let you go."

The comments were coming rapid-fire during the two-hour fort tour, followed by more of the same at an afternoon cocktail party, and then that evening during the cruise's last formal dinner. What exactly had Saul told his traveling companions?

After the closing dinner ended, he and I made our way back along the cobblestone streets to the hotel where I had spent the evening alone the night before. Just one more day until we got on the boat to sail.

The hotel room had a balcony and porch overlooking a large lawn leading down to the water. Sitting in rocking chairs watching the moonbeams dance in the sunlight was serene and relaxing.

"I can't wait to sail around the world with you," Saul gushed.

My stomach rose to my throat.

"Saul," I stammered. "I must remind you of the premise of this trip. You told me you wanted me to see your sailing world so I could understand what you care about. Here I am. As lovely as it sounds, I'm not prepared to sail around the world with you. Remember that I told you I plan to see other people this summer. You'll be gone for three more months, and as you know, I just started dating a month ago."

Leaping from his chair, he glared at me, his face a mask of fury. "How dare you embarrass me in front of my friends like this? What?! You just plan to 'sample' other men until you find the one you like?

Am I not good enough for you? I told you I made an exception to date you. You live too far away, you didn't go to an Ivy League school, you've had cancer so you might die, and now you say you want to date other people?!"

"Saul," I said, as gently as I could manage. "I'll stay here for this week if you want to show me your sailing life. But my conditions are what I spelled out when I said yes."

At that, Saul stalked off the balcony into the bedroom, got into bed with his clothes on, and turned out the light. From the porch, I could hear his ear-shattering snore. All night long I laid awake, questioning if I hadn't been direct enough, or if I had been unfair.

The next morning, I restated my thoughts:

"Saul, I think it's time for me to get on a plane and go back to New York. Do you agree?"

Still fuming with white rage, Saul muttered slowly through clenched teeth: "You might as well learn to sail."

"Okay, I'll stay," I answered. "As long as you understand how I see this."

Early the next morning on our first day at sea, I got violently sick as the boat began moving. Shaking and retching in the head of the sleeping quarters below deck, I didn't have the strength to stand. Saul came to check on me when I didn't appear on deck. Mortified that he had to undress me out of my pajamas, get me into foul weather gear, and practically carry me from the cabin, I knew then I wasn't cut out for the sailing life.

Up on deck, I sat still for hours, swathed in blankets as the wind blew and the boat rocked over the heavy pitch of the waves. Six hours later, I could finally nibble on crackers and take a sip of Coke.

Whether he took pity or not, Saul didn't go easy on me for the rest of the week. I learned sailing vocabulary, how to steer the boat, coil and stow the lines, call out commands to help guide the dinghy to shore, and cook on a tiny stovetop below deck.

I learned that Saul's friends are lovely people. I learned Sweden's washers and dryers are eco-friendly and take seven hours to do three loads. I learned Sweden is beautiful in the summer. I learned I'll never be a sailor.

And I learned I could make an exception for a week with a man who thought he was making an exception for me.

Best of all, I learned I was still me when I got on that flight to come home. And that finally, I could sleep sitting up on a plane after all.

LEVI the Lawyer

♫ Love the One You're With ♫

Artist: Stephen Sills

Years of living in Texas accustomed me to eating certain kinds of food, prepared in traditional ways. Hamburger, nachos, chicken fried steak, mac and cheese, green salad with ranch dressing, and brisket were available on almost every menu.

When I moved to New York, all of my customary culinary preferences were unrecognizable.

Chicken breasts were now chicken cutlets. Durkees mustard was nowhere to be found. Condiments didn't ever include jalapenos. Barbecue was a noun, not a verb. New York pizza was a separate food group. And like believing in Santa Claus, there really was a neighborhood bagel store.

When I matched on Coffee Meets Bagel with Levi, whose profile included photos of a mammoth outdoor grill laden with seafood and potatoes, my taste buds watered.

Levi either liked to eat or cook, or both. Either way, I wanted to be the beneficiary.

On our first phone call, Levi and I discovered we had lots in common.

- an affection for food, both prepared at home and eaten out.
- an appreciation for many types of music.
- interest in museum going.
- a love of travel.
- enjoyment in reading books.
- a fascination with puns and the English language.

- an appetite for adventure.
- navigating the parenting of young adult daughters close to the same age.

And we had our differences.

- Levi is an Ivy League educated lawyer; I took the LSAT, but never went to law school.
- Levi is an economist and an expert in the futures market; what I thought I knew about my future got blown wide open by the move to New York.
- Levi was a long-haired hippie in his youth; I have never even smoked a cigarette.
- Levi studied in China; I like Chinese food.
- Levi is a practicing Jew; I grew up Catholic and my uncle was a priest.
- Levi likes Scotch neat; I am a neat person.
- Levi doesn't like to dance; dance floors don't scare me.
- Levi likes his Fiat; I love my SUV.
- Levi goes to bed early; I stay up late.
- Levi plays the ukulele; I play the piano.
- Levi states facts; I tell stories.
- Levi deletes every text message; I keep them all.

"I am willing to take a bet on you," Levi said at the end of our call. "How about dinner in a few days? I live in Scarsdale and commute into the City for work. My law firm's office is in the building next door to Grand Central Terminal. We can meet at the Oyster Bar for dinner. It's on the lower level of the station. Good food, classic NY."

Our thirty-minute phone call took place on Saturday afternoon. We set our date for the next Thursday night.

On Sunday, the day after we talked by phone, Levi sent a text:

"Looking forward to dinner. How was your day? I went to the gym, did some reading, went to the Cooper-Hewitt Museum in the City, and did some experimental grilling on the barbecue."

An accompanying photo featured jumbo cooked shrimp, artfully arranged on a decorative platter.

"Yum!" I answered. "Save some for me."

"They were a hit and are all gone. But you can dine on shrimp to your heart's content at the Oyster Bar. Let me know what you are wearing, day of."

On Thursday morning, I sent Levi a message:

"Hi, Levi, I look forward to tonight. I am wearing a navy pantsuit, cream top, with a pink necklace as a one-off reference to Texas."

"Kate, looking forward to it. Like everyone else, I'll be in a gray pinstripe suit with a blue tie."

At 7 PM that evening, I arrived at the Oyster Bar's entrance and spoke to the maitre d' at the front.

"Hello, I am joining Mr. Solomon," I announced, when I heard a voice across the foyer.

"Kate, I am Levi," said a serious-looking man standing off to the side.

"Oh, hi," I smiled, turning, and extending my hand.

His handshake was all business. Through thick-rimmed glasses, Levi looked at me quizzically as if assessing a potential juror.

"Good to meet you," I said.

"This way," he gestured as he followed the host. I fell in step behind them.

The dining room was an enormous warren of brightly lit rooms, spanned by a domed ceiling of blond wood. Tables were covered in red and white checked cloths, and waiters with thick menus in black binders tucked under their arms scurried back and forth. Busboys hustled to clear the tables, loading huge serving trays with platters of empty oyster shells, and resetting white dinner plates and napkin-rolled silverware.

Part business crowd, part commuters, part tourists, the place was crackling with energy and noise.

Levi and I were seated right in the middle of the main dining room at a two-top table. The service was swift. A waiter handed him the menus, as a busboy poured water, and a captain rushed by, casting a quick supervisory look our way.

In a decisive voice and with a thin smile in my direction, Levi immediately told the waiter to bring us a shrimp cocktail. Then he handed me my menu. Paging through it, I quickly saw the selection was overwhelming.

"Would you order for me, please?" I asked. "Anything except mussels or octopus. I haven't worked up to those yet."

"A pity," he said with a serious expression. "We will just have to bring you along." And then the corners of his mouth turned up, and the business-like veneer cracked ever so slightly.

I wonder if this man laughs, I thought to myself, as he studiously read the menu.

"All set. I will surprise you," he announced, slapping the menu shut.

The meal of grilled fish and vegetables was delicious. Even more than the food, I focused on the conversation.

Prompted by my questioning, Levi told me about his family,

former marriage, and dating life. Single for almost a decade, he had recently experienced a serious breakup. Now, he was testing the waters again.

"What are you really looking for?" I asked, as our evening drew to a close.

"It's simple," he said. "I have a lot of interests and I want to share them. I want a woman who has time to be with me. I do go out a lot, both for work and socially. But I also want company when I am at home. Let's put it this way: I want a woman who would prefer to go to Home Depot with me on a Friday night, than to the opera with somebody else. And until I find her, I'll keep meeting new people and getting to know them. I never eat alone."

"Well, thank you for treating me to dinner tonight," I responded, completely unsure what grade I had earned on his dating report card.

Returning to the restaurant foyer on our way out, I turned to Levi. "Close your eyes," I said, as I held out my two closed fists. "Which hand?" I asked.

"Left," he said, looking more annoyed than curious.

"Right, you are!" I answered, opening my hand to reveal a shiny penny. "I always pick them up," I went on. "They're for good luck. I found this one in Grand Central today. Here, you take it."

He pocketed the penny.

We parted with a handshake and a quick hug. He went one way to catch his train to Scarsdale, and I headed for the street to catch a taxi.

Inside the car, I texted my thanks.

"Levi, I'm so glad we had dinner tonight. Thanks again for meeting and treating me. You are a great conversationalist and an even better listener. I look forward to seeing you again. Take care of that lucky penny I found at Irving Roasters in Grand Central today."

"Hah, what were you doing there? Afraid I wouldn't feed you?" he asked. "Never mind. I will keep it safe. I always want the fates on my side. I had a great time and look forward to seeing you again."

At the beginning of the next week, Levi got in touch to ask about my plans for the weekend. I explained I already had a trip scheduled back to Texas.

"No worries re timing. Feel free to share your doings and random thoughts by text in the interim. And if you ever need a date for one of your events, I'm available for rent and clean up well. Have a good day. L."

During my travels, Levi stayed in touch:

"I just survived a not-for-profit's annual gala, making the 9:42 PM train home by a hair. How do you stand going to these things as much as I assume you do? The live auction and the process of squeezing attendees for donations make me queasy. How was your day? L."

"Sounds like you made it out unscathed in spite of your distaste for such gatherings," I answered back. "Do you also dislike the small talk?"

"No, small talk is my specialty," Levi responded, "as long as I can be in control of when it ends."

"I am sorry I am not there to experience this," I exclaimed. "Give me an example."

"My pitching style: direct, no hype. I don't embellish with many words," Levi offered. "How'd your Texas visit go? Time with your daughter? When do you resurface in NY? I've been very busy with work. Went to a firm dinner at the Plaza tonight. I hate those things. Too much banality, no substance. I escaped early. Looking forward to Father's Day with my girls. I'll cook for them," he ended his rapid-fire text thoughts.

"From all you've told me. I bet you are a terrific dad to your girls. I believe the most pivotal developmental gift a father can provide a daughter is unconditional love."

"Thanks. I wish I had taught them to clean up better!" Levi quipped.

"Themselves or the dishes?" I asked.

"Dishes, their rooms, etc. My youngest daughter is living with me right now. I just shut the door to her bedroom."

"So, when am I going to get a chance to see how well YOU clean up after those delicious meals you prepare?" I asked. "Maybe your daughter and I could both lend a hand."

"You'd have to come to Scarsdale for the experience," he said. "And it would be a better plan if you were here at a time she wasn't... for a number of reasons. How about this coming weekend? I will cook for you when you get back. But first, let me take you to lunch in Manhattan. Then you can see how my cooking compares."

The next week, I met Levi at La Fonda Del Sol, a clubby business restaurant in the MET Life Building between Grand Central and his law firm's office building. I arrived early, wearing a plum-colored shift dress and black heels. The hostess smiled when she heard I was waiting for Mr. Solomon.

"Right this way," she said.

"He must be a regular then," I stated, hoping for a response.

"Indeed," she said cryptically as she gave me the option of where to sit. I chose a burgundy leather banquette facing into the dining room. Tall paneled wood mirrors accented the wall behind me and shined prisms of light onto the tables.

From my vantage point, I could see the entire room. Although the restaurant was almost at capacity, the decibel level of conversations seemed hushed. The thick carpet and richly appointed furnishings buffered the sound.

I smiled at Levi as he walked up the three steps from the bar into the dining room. Removing his suit coat, he leaned down and kissed me on the cheek. I could see him relax as he placed the coat on his chair, across from my seat on the banquette.

Our conversation was easy—my trip, his work, what was going on in the news. As our entrée plates were cleared away, Levi leaned back in his chair and looked at me with what was by now a familiar hybrid half-serious/half-playful expression.

"So, shall we plan for dinner at my place? My daughter Susie will be away this weekend. All you have to do is get yourself there. It's easy by train," he explained.

"I actually have a car," I said. "I'll drive to you. That way you can avoid any interruption to your cooking by having to pick me up at the train station. I wouldn't want to be responsible for burned sauce."

"I was going to make you walk," he said, as we were standing up to go. Looking down at my heels, he tsked. "But those shoes would not do. I walk every day to and from the Scarsdale train, but never in heels."

"Well, then you don't have to worry about me breaking an ankle, and you having to carry me the rest of the way," I said. "What can I bring?"

"I never ask my guests to contribute to the meal. Just bring your sparkling personality," he answered as he looked me carefully up and down. "And I would never carry you. Call an ambulance first."

The day before my drive to Scarsdale, Levi sent a text:

"Do you eat lamb chops or steak, or would you prefer fish or seafood?"

"You're serious about cooking, aren't you? Please surprise me again. I completely trust your gustatory judgment!"

"What else do you trust?" he asked.

"Should I not have a reason to trust you?" I inquired.

"I am a lawyer, remember. I never go on record."

On Sunday morning, the day of my dinner at Levi's, I awoke feeling under the weather. It was my first time to be sick since moving to New York. I didn't know if I was contagious.

"Hi, Levi," I messaged him. "I woke up with head congestion and all that goes with it. I am still very much game to be there if you aren't put off by a husky voice. Just let me know what you think."

"Come!" was the immediate answer.

When I pulled up in front of Levi's home hours later, it was my first introduction to the affluent town of Scarsdale. An upscale semirural enclave of professionals, the village neighborhoods are beautiful.

Levi's two-story home was on a quiet leafy corner, a Mediterranean style with a red French tile roof. An iron banister on the second floor framed an upstairs balcony which ran the entire length of the front of the house.

Set on a steep hill, the home had at least twenty steps to the beveled glass front door. Manicured flower beds and plantings of flowering trees were a handsome accent to the hilly lawn.

Parking in front of the house was an option, but I didn't relish the climb up the steps to ring the doorbell.

Exploring other options, I drove around the corner where the elevation was more forgiving. Unsure where to put my car, I pulled in behind a Fiat in the driveway.

Another iron railing bordered a patio, covered on one side with an inviting outdoor furniture arrangement, and open on the opposite side to a sliding glass door. At just that moment, Levi came out of the door wearing an apron, carrying an enormous platter of food in one hand, and pushing his glasses back on his nose with the other.

The top of a gleaming silver barbecue grill was open, no doubt the same one in the photo I had spotted on his dating profile. I walked up the flagstone path, climbed the few steps to reach the patio, and called out to him.

"I didn't see you," Levi said, waving a spatula. He looked less like the master of the house in his apron, and more like a helpful clerk at an overstocked hardware store.

"How can I help?" I asked.

"I like to do things my way," he announced, no surprise. "But I put out some appetizers for you," he said, motioning to the table.

It was a cornucopia of treats. Prosciutto. Hard cheese. Salami. Endive leaves. Two kinds of olives. And giant radishes.

"Save room for lamb and chicken, corn on the cob, and Brussels sprouts," Levi called over his shoulder as I took a plate.

"Are you kidding? This is a feast!" I said appreciatively.

"Excellent!" (I was to learn that was one of his favorite words.)

The captain in charge refused to have me assist at the grill. Once inside the house's expansive kitchen, I tried again.

"Okay, you can peel the corn. The water's almost ready, and outside is under control. By the way, I intend to kiss you while the corn is boiling," Levi said in his half-smiling way.

"Is that so? Well then, let me get moving."

No sooner had I plopped the ears of corn into the sputtering water, than he was behind me.

"Might as well," he said as he kissed me, first perfunctorily, and then with greater intention. We pulled apart after a few moments, and he immediately went back to his cooking chores. It was as if he had checked a box in a seduction scene (kiss her first!) and then back to work.

I slipped into the powder room, past a winding staircase in the main hallway, to check my lipstick. Not too much smudged, I saw, as I considered the aphrodisiac powers of lamb on Levi.

Heading back to the kitchen, I glanced at my surroundings. The living room and adjacent sitting room were cleanly furnished in Craftsman style. The home was definitely a man's. Dark leather couches, simple window treatments, and uncluttered spaces defined the look.

Purchases from Levi's many Asian travels were on display, as well as samples of his handmade pottery creations. His photographic art adorned the walls. I made a mental note to ask for a tour.

Back outside, I noshed on appetizers and enjoyed the summer evening. It was dark now, and fireflies were everywhere. The glass of red wine he offered me added to the tranquil mood.

Over dinner, our conversation revolved around my perspective about life in New York, especially as compared to Texas.

Levi chimed in.

"If asked to describe you, it would be impossible to miss the obvious Texas pedigree: good clothes, big hair, big personality. But underneath that Texas charm thing, there's something else. It's a no-apologies fierce determination. So, my nickname for you is going to be FC."

"FC?" I said, puzzled.

"Yes, FC," he answered as he took a sip of wine. "It stands for

'Fucking Commando'. I can already see when you set your mind to something, you make it happen."

"It's either that nickname or Croutons," he went on, "since you consumed every one of them. "You pick." he offered.

"I'm flattered to be called FC," I said. "I'll need to live up to my reputation, though."

"As long as you do it ethically," he answered. "Hate to have to visit you in prison!"

"Oh, is that where FC's go when they take their roles too seriously?" I kidded.

"If they don't register with the SEC like they should!" Levi extended the metaphor to incorporate his knowledge of government regulatory agencies. "We need to discuss what happens when you don't comply."

"Oh, I would never register . . . so what happens?" I bantered.

"There could be appropriate punishments for that badness," he said dryly.

"Surely you could give me a hint as to what they are . . . maybe I should register after all."

"Yes, indeed," he said. "Step this way."

Levi stood up from his chair at the patio table and walked to the outdoor furniture grouping. Taking a seat on the couch, he patted the cushion next to him.

"Anyone who eats my corn with such relish may get a dispensation on the punishment for misbehaving. Come closer, and we can talk about it."

As I sat down, he pulled me closer and began to kiss me aggressively.

"We can do this here, or go inside so we don't shock the neighbors," he said after a few minutes.

"Oh, I don't mind the neighbors if they don't mind us," I replied.

"I do believe they might mind what I have in mind."

"Are you suggesting my new nickname might have a double meaning?" I inquired.

"Perhaps," he said, standing up, and taking my hand to pull me off the couch.

"What about the dishes?" I asked.

"You are a mood killer," he responded.

"You are a lawyer, and I know you like to get things done. So, let's do the dishes."

While Levi cleaned the grill, I carried everything to the kitchen. I could sense he was happy to get the tasks completed, even though I had disrupted his earlier plan.

Back inside, his mood from our outside escapade was waning, and I gratefully prepared to take my leave and drive home.

"What are you doing next weekend?" he asked.

"I'm excited to have a girlfriend coming in from Texas. We're going to a Broadway show on Saturday night."

"I'm going to a Broadway show on Saturday night too," he said, hesitatingly.

"Ah, fascinating," I responded. "I thought you were an opera guy, and that Broadway held absolutely no interest for you."

He looked uncomfortable.

"The FC in me emboldens me to ask what you are seeing," I went on.

"Well, I got tickets for *Dear Evan Hanson* quite some time ago," Levi hedged.

"Really?! Where are you sitting? That's the show my friend and I are seeing!" I responded, both stunned at the coincidence and amused by his discomfort.

Levi left the room and came back with the tickets. I typed his row and seat numbers into a note on my phone.

"Great," I said enthusiastically. "When I get home, I'll text my friend. She got the tickets through her special connection at the box office, so I'm hoping they are good seats. I'll let you know where they are. And then I'll look forward to seeing you at the theater next weekend."

He looked even more uncomfortable.

And then I knew. He had a date.

"Ah, I get it now," I said. "Chalk it up to my FC powers of discernment," I went on, trying to lighten the mood.

"Well, we can say hello. It will be strictly professional," I said, confidently. I already imagined how interesting it would be to see who he was with and how they behaved together.

"Sure, we can do that," he said, though not very convincingly.

Before I made it home, Levi had sent a message.

"I've been thinking about how much I enjoyed being with you. Given your friend's visit next weekend, I'm sorry we have to wait so long to explore further. Sorry about weirdness re Saturday night. Amazing. Awkward, but will work out."

The week flew by before my Saturday evening of crossing paths with Levi and his date. My friend was very excited about being a conspiratorial party to the theater meeting. She and I both narrowed down his likely date prospects to a few of his female followers on Instagram.

It was no secret that Levi and I were dating other people. But even so, in a city of 8 million people, the theater rendezvous was a true long-shot coincidence, in equal measure as fascinating as it was surprising. The stars were aligning for a sure run-in.

Although the Music Box Theater where the show was performed has a seating capacity of just over a thousand, the orchestra level feels intimate. Organized with two aisles separating the seating sections, seats to the left and right of center are just eight deep.

The tickets my friend secured were in house right. So were Levi's . . . in the row directly in front of us! I would have an unobstructed view of him throughout the performance.

When I discovered where I was sitting in the theater, I did not share the information with Levi. It was a planned sin of omission. He would have no idea if or when our theater encounter would take place. And I wanted to keep it that way. Not only would I get an unguarded reaction, but I would also have the FC advantage.

After a quick dinner, my friend and I arrived early for the show. I took the seat on the aisle. Levi and his date would have to walk past us to go into the row in front and then move eight seats to the wall. I intended to stand up and greet him when they came in.

Curtain was at 8 PM. My friend and I had been in our seats since 7:30 PM. Thirty minutes before curtain and the theater was filling up.

7:45 PM No sighting of him. A little strange, as I had come to know Levi as precisely punctual.

7:50 PM Still no sighting. The row in front of me was full except for his two seats.

7:55 PM Still no Levi. Announcements were being made about turning off cell phones and advising the audience to be seated for the start of the show.

7:59 PM Finally, I spotted him! Levi and his date had just entered the theater, but from the side wings. He had forced her to crawl around a post to climb into their seats at the end of the row. At best, it was a creative way to enter the theater. At worst, it was a calculated move.

Throughout the first half of the show, I was preoccupied thinking about the moment of truth when we would run into each other at intermission. There was no way he could avoid me. The theater was too small, and he was seated too close.

I was wrong.

As soon as the curtain went down for intermission, Levi hurried his date out the way they had come in and disappeared. Where had they gone? They returned only seconds before the curtain went up, the same way they had entered at the start.

Now I was irritated. He had gone out of his way to avoid me, despite our agreeing we would say hello. I was more intent than ever to bump into him when the show was over.

My friend and I had a plan. Guessing Levi and his date would exit from the side wings at curtain, we cut across our row headed for the same exit to beat them at their game.

What Levi hadn't counted on was that leaving from the side wings would dump him right back into the lobby where my friend and I were waiting. As the crowd poured out of the theater exits, milled into the lobby, and then spilled onto the sidewalk outside, I looked but didn't see him.

"How is it possible we missed him?" I said incredulously to my friend.

And then I saw him, standing smack dab in front of me. We were face-to-face. Levi looked perplexed and pale, squaring his back to block his date, standing behind him, from seeing me.

I gave him a hard glare and walked away.

The next morning, Levi sent a text message at 7:26 AM:

"Good morning! I hope you liked the show as much as I did. I didn't feel shortchanged by the understudies. I thought it was really creative and the characters were very real. I liked the moral ambiguity. I look forward to discussing it with you. How has your weekend been with your friend? I liked your photo yesterday on Instagram.

I got in a bike ride, swim, food shopping trip, and a nap. All in all, it was a great day. I think I might go sailing this afternoon."

I waited several hours and then sent a carefully considered response.

"Good morning, Levi,

When I think about recapping my Saturday, the first thing that comes to mind isn't sending you a text reporting on yesterday as an ordinary day. Last night we were faced with a "one in a million" extraordinary situation.

Yes, I am comfortable with the "don't ask, don't tell" policy on dating others. Yet, we knew that being in the same place at the same time was going to happen. And given the direction that our most recent date was headed, the complication of last night could not have been without forethought for either of us.

That you didn't mention any discomfort on your part, or acknowledge any of mine, was quite surprising. That you went to extraordinary measures to avoid me at the theater was disingenuous. Even a wave hello could have worked.

And if we had said hello, we had agreed we would keep it professional. At minimum, my Texas friend had heard a lot about you, and couldn't understand why you chose to avoid her too.

Your not acknowledging me was disappointing. Maybe we had our own moral ambiguity.

I'm glad you had a good day yesterday. Enjoy sailing. I look forward to talking to you soon."

Within the hour, Levi answered back:

"Kate, sorry that I made a challenging situation more difficult. There was no roadmap on how to handle it. I have real affection and respect for you and would not want to behave towards you in any way that would make you feel bad. If you want to chat, between 2 PM and 4 PM would work for me. Enjoy your day."

I called Levi during the allotted time window.

"Did no woman ever teach you how to flirt?" I began. "If so, you could have pulled it off last night. I do give you major props for the apology, even though I had to extract it out of you. But that's what an FC does! I know one thing for sure," I went on. "I was having WAY more fun than you last night. It's sort of like the difference between thinking about boiling the corn and actually doing it. Where there's predetermination, there might actually be a crime."

Levi laughed softly into the phone. "Kate, for a neophyte just getting started in the dating world, you take no prisoners."

"Thank you for the compliment," I answered. "Like you, I am navigating how to date more than one person. Last night is a good tutorial on what not to do. I wanted to address it so we can both learn from the experience. It appears we have."

"Yes," said Levi. "I am taking out the sackcloth and ashes you Catholics use for penitence. On a happier thought, I'd like to keep seeing you as long as we both mutually enjoy it. The proper lawyer in me can't allow myself to type the exact thoughts, but I see Michelin prospects in you."

"I am always going to have FC standards," I emphasized.

"I will do my best to keep up with you!" he said. "I see you can teach me more than a few things. Your candor is why people want to stay in your life. Brutal honesty with Southern Belle charm. For some people, I am sure that's confusing. For me, that's excitement."

"For a lawyer to admit vulnerability is the first step to a better world." I reflected. "A world of transparent attorneys and a lot of fresh boiled corn."

EZRA the Entrepreneur

♪ Magic Carpet Ride ♪

Artist: Steppenwolf

In his online profile photo, he stood tall. Very tall. And the camel brown leather shoes he wore were a sophisticated pairing with a navy jacket, lavender shirt and rep tie, and khaki slacks. His look said professional, but not stodgy. And the sparkle in his dark eyes, set behind an almost invisible pair of high fashion eyeglasses, captivated me.

So I messaged him.

"Found you," I said. "Except that it appears you're somewhere over Canadian soil from the GPS locator on this dating site. However, if you ever set foot in New York, I'd like to say hello!"

Within several hours I got a message back.

"You caught me. I'm traveling cross country, but I actually live in New Jersey and can't wait to give you a call."

We exchanged numbers, always my practice with anyone I am interested in getting to know. No risk, no gain.

His area code confirmed he lived at least reasonably near me. But it was anybody's guess if I would ever hear from him.

A few days later, I was sitting cross-legged on the floor of my entry hall, sorting through yet another shipping box I hadn't unpacked after my recent move to New York. This one contained framed photos that had once been in my home and office in Texas. Most of the images were of my daughter from the time she was a little girl . . . playing with pots and pans in the kitchen, waiting in line to ride Space Mountain at Disney World, or singing carols by the piano at Christmas.

Unwrapping every tissue-covered picture frame was a reminder of how much my new existence was a major departure from my old life. Then I was part of a family and an established community. Here I was single and alone, building a different life, one new friend at a time.

My cell phone rang and interrupted the reverie.

"Hi, Kate, this is Ezra. Good time to speak?"

The juxtaposition of talking to an unfamiliar voice—against the backdrop of being buried in a box of photos from my former life—was jolting.

Switching to methodically folding the packing paper that held the photos, instead of walking down memory lane, I answered brightly:

"Sure," I said.

"What are you doing?" he asked.

"Sitting on the floor of my hallway buried in tissue paper. I just moved to New York, and it seems I can always find another box to unpack."

"That's exciting!" he said, seeming to mean it. "Have you discovered anything that surprised you?" His immediate thoughtfulness in asking me not only what I was doing, but also about its significance, was refreshing.

"More than you know, "I said. "I think my life is flashing in front of me."

He laughed deeply with a sincere warmth to the sound. "I believe we bring our energy with us, no matter what we do. I can hear it in your voice."

"Actually, I already know you are amazing," he said, completely taking me aback.

"How?" I asked. "I read about you," he said. "I think you're like me. We are out-of-the-box thinkers. I want to know more about you, Kate."

His fascinating accent added emphasis to his words. I couldn't quite get it. It wasn't northeastern United States, and it wasn't European. But it was melodic and rich, and his confidence and boldness gave it more power.

"Ezra, tell me where you're from."

"Israel originally, but I have been in the U.S. a long time."

"So, what are you looking for?" he asked directly. "I am talking to you on a mission. I am attracted to your courage. I think dating is a dance. You do what you feel. I like to test the limits. I always ask what's the point. We are here to enjoy life. So, when do I get to enjoy you?"

"Wow, you get right to it, don't you?" I countered. "I am off on a trip next week, but after that, I'll be here."

"Are you going with a man?" he asked.

Organizing my thoughts, I answered. "Well, as a matter of fact, I'm dating different people and have been invited to learn how to sail next week with one of them."

"Thanks for being honest with me," he said. "I imagine you have a lot of people interested in you. But I think I'm going to be able to sweep you off your feet, and so I'll patiently wait until you get back. But don't be surprised if I call you while you're gone. That okay?"

When the conversation ended thirty minutes later, I felt I had been seduced on the phone. Ezra's bold, get it done approach was refreshingly direct, if not a bit intimidating. And I was curious to see how it would play out.

True to his word, Ezra called me while I was on my trip. Catching me alone my first night in the hotel, he spoke excitedly of the plans for our first date, which we had agreed to schedule for the night after I got back from the trip.

He was taking me to dinner—wherever I wanted to go—and to see *Hamilton*, the hottest musical on Broadway. Since he was traveling in from New Jersey, he announced he would be staying in a hotel in New York City. With a view. Looking out on Central Park. Would I care to join him?

Ezra could hear the hesitation in my voice about the offer of shared accommodations. And by the plans for such an over-the-top first date. A million thoughts ran through my mind. Was this going to be amazing or odd? Should I be concerned he might harm me? Could I get references?!

"I know you are worried," he said, as if picking up on my unspoken musings. "But there's no reason to be. I'm a perfect gentleman and I respect your honor. If there's anything you don't like, you can certainly leave. No funny business. I promise.

I want to wine and dine you and tell you that you are beautiful. Miracles don't just happen. We create them. The universe listens to us. Stay with me. We will have the next morning for breakfast and a walk around the park before we each have to go back to our lives."

He paused, and I was silent.

"Join me?" he asked.

"Yes," I said, still not entirely sure, but excited at the possibilities.

The date with Ezra occupied a lot of my thoughts during the sailing trip. As soon as I returned to New York City, I got a call from him confirming our plans for the next night.

"Good evening, my princess," he said excitedly. "I can't wait to see you. Wear something that shows off your figure. Let's meet at the hotel first before we go to dinner."

Packing the next morning stumped me. What do I take? How can I plan for such an unscripted and potentially romantic 20 hours? Am I crazy for even doing this?

Finally, with an overnight bag organized, I got ready. I wore a sleeveless straight black square neck dress, cinched with wide bands of yellow and royal blue stripes at the waist. My black patent shoes had kitten heels, flattering enough for the dress and good for walking in the City.

It was summer, and the weather was perfect. On the ride to the hotel, I kept the taxi windows down to better see all the views of the City. Although I was a resident, I was also a forever tourist, soaking it all in.

The Essex House hotel is directly across from Central Park. Horse drawn carriages were lined up across the street, ready to transport riders into the park. Bicyclists weaved in and out of the cars. And the street bustled with tourists and locals out on foot to soak in the beautiful afternoon.

Exiting the taxi, I pulled my small bag into the elegant lobby. Ezra was waiting by a round entry table that held a towering display of flowers under an enormous crystal chandelier. Standing at 6' 5", he cut an imposing figure. There was no way I was going to miss him.

With a giant smile and those friendly deep-brown eyes I had seen in his photos, he took two long steps to get to me, circling his arms around me in an all-engulfing bear hug. I reached up to avoid getting suffocated.

"Wow! Just let me look at you," Ezra said, extending back, and pushing me gently away. He glanced up and down my body, not in a leering way, but with approval and appreciation. "You don't disappoint," he murmured, taking my suitcase with one hand and putting his arm around my waist with the other.

"Let's go upstairs for a few minutes. I have something to show you, and we have time before our dinner reservations," he said, not so much asking, but instead announcing what was on the agenda next.

The elevator moved quietly and swiftly to the 30th floor, and Ezra took my hand to lead me to the room. The magnetic key opened the door with a soft click, and my attention first went to the dresser.

A giant vase with more red roses than I could count stood in the center, nestled by at least a dozen votive candles, positioned next to a wine cooler. Oh my!

A bottle of chilled champagne, two crystal glasses, and a bowl of strawberries were waiting.

And beyond that, past my view of the dresser and the bed, was a full-length couch, upholstered in navy velvet with rope trim, and centered in an expansive window. Just beyond the back of the couch was a breathtaking view of Central Park.

Usually afraid of heights, I walked to the window and peered down. Below me was a carpet of green as far as the eye could see, surrounded by countless high-rise buildings rimming the park's perimeter on the north, east, and west sides.

I sucked in a deep breath and turned to him. "You did all this for me?"

"Yes, my dear. And I can see you're going to be worth it!"

And with that, he popped the champagne cork and poured two glasses. We clinked them. He smiled, and we each took a sip.

We made small talk as we were drinking the champagne, although it was admittedly surreal to be standing in a hotel bedroom with a man I had just met moments before. He must have had a similar thought as he gestured towards the couch. Grateful for a place to sit besides the bed, I chose a corner of the three-cushion sofa.

Because he was such a big man, it didn't take but a slight movement for Ezra to pull me over to him with a smile.

"This is going to be a beautiful night!" he proclaimed.

Ezra looked handsome in a long-sleeve blue Tattersall shirt, dress slacks, and rich brown Oxford shoes. He had worn the business attire for me.

With my Texas roots, I was used to being dressed up, even by New York standards. When we discussed intended attire for the evening, he had confessed he normally didn't get dressed up for dates. But he would for me.

Now, he was gazing approvingly at me, and I was thinking getting dressed up hadn't been such a bad idea. I smiled and took another sip of champagne.

"May I kiss you?" he asked as if he didn't expect a no. And without waiting for an answer, he leaned in and softly touched his lips to mine.

"Ah," he sighed happily. "When two people meet, there's always the human factor. It's the difference-maker. It's chemistry. We have it!"

Between the kisses, the strawberries, a box of chocolates he produced from a bedside table, and my sips of champagne, I wasn't sure at that moment I was in any position to disagree!

By the time we left for dinner, I had abandoned the thought that I could be in danger and instead embraced what lay ahead. The small continental restaurant in the Theater District that Ezra chose was charming, if not a bit distractingly loud.

His very tall frame made him oversized for our two-top table. Without complaint, he extended his legs into the aisle to secure enough balance on the small wooden chair that crested at his mid-back. Immersed in a detailed conversation about our lives, we enjoyed a delicious meal of succulent steamed vegetables, rotisserie chicken, followed by flaming bananas Foster. Even though he had to feel cramped, Ezra didn't seem uncomfortable in the least.

But after dinner and back outside on the sidewalk, he stretched to his full height. "That feels good," he said. Circling both arms around my waist, he pulled me back to him, and took a selfie on his phone. Flattered that he wanted to document the evening so early on, and flush with wine from dinner, I leaned my head against his shoulder. My goofy grin in the photo revealed my 'devil may care' attitude.

My head cleared as we walked the few blocks to the Richard Rodgers Theatre. The air outside crackled with excitement as the crowd lined up to gain admission to the building. Once inside, we mingled with the sold-out crowd, excited to see the most popular show on the Great White Way.

Hamilton lived up to the hype. Even though I had seen the show once before, I was still captivated the second time around. Admittedly, I also couldn't stop thinking of what was going to happen after the play.

Throughout the performance, Ezra held my hand, touched my leg, and stole frequent glances at my profile. Due to his large frame, he sat physically closer to me than the small confines of a theater seat would typically impose. And seated, he towered over me. I felt sorry for the person who tried to watch the show behind us!

When we stood together to take part in the standing ovation, I was glad to be in heels. Even so, the extra few inches I gained with my footwear were no match for his height. To return Ezra's unabashed grins at me, I looked up towards the breathtaking medallions in the ceiling.

Awash in the glow of the evening's performance, we departed the theater on a high.

"What about a carriage ride in Central Park?" he asked.

"You are an incurable romantic!" I exclaimed. "How could I say no?"

The evening had turned chilly, and I was grateful for the thick blanket Ezra placed over our laps as the horse pulled away from the curb. Our carriage was all red, with red leather cushions and red carnation flowers. A red leather plume adorned the horse's bridle halter.

The steady clip-clop of hooves on the pavement was punctuated with the whispered encouraging murmur from the driver to his steed. Twinkling lights illuminating New York City skyscrapers, the glow of lamps casting shadows in Central Park, and the natural beauty of the park's surroundings were mesmerizing. I was truly sorry when the ride ended thirty minutes later.

We came to a stop directly across from the hotel. It was almost midnight. I was feeling slightly weary—the return from my weeklong sailing trip had taken a toll, and the anticipatory adrenaline buildup for this date had now been depleted by champagne, wine, and the highs of dinner, theater, and the carriage ride.

"Let's head to the room," Ezra said, guiding me to the elevator. Then it hit me. This man was wide awake, and we were going back to a room with roses and chocolates. I wasn't sure sleep was on the agenda!

I'm still not certain how he pulled it off, but there was now a chocolate cake, china plates, linen napkins, and more chilled champagne when we arrived back at the room. And the candles were lit.

It occurred to me that he had made friends with the hotel staff who assisted him in creating luxurious and captivating first dates. And it also occurred to me that maybe I had agreed to be dessert!

The cake was delicious, decadent, and dream-inducing. After a giant slice and a half (and another glass of champagne), I happily kicked off my shoes and laid sideways on the bed.

Four hours later I awoke, fully clothed, under the covers, and laying with my head on the pillow. Ezra was sound asleep beside me.

I quietly slipped out of bed. Once inside the large marble bathroom, I closed the door behind me and removed my clothes. Luxuriating in a long hot shower, I reflected on the most remarkable first date I had ever had. Whether it ended the way Ezra intended or not, I didn't know. But I was grateful to have at least gotten some sleep.

Slipping back into bed, now dressed in pajamas, I quietly put my head on the pillow and pulled the blankets close. The room was freezing with the air conditioning going full blast—clearly Ezra's preferred sleeping temperature. He was snoring deeply. Good, I thought. More sleep for me. A perfect conclusion to an evening full of promise.

When the date ended after brunch on Sunday, Ezra was already talking about the future. He wanted to take me to Israel. He wanted to show me his home in Morristown, New Jersey. He wanted to introduce me to his work colleagues, his children, and to his favorite Israeli restaurant in a small village near his home.

The next Friday, while I was at work, I got a call from my next-door neighbor. "I have a surprise for you. Come by on your way home," she said.

Waiting for me there was the most gorgeous bouquet I had ever seen. Sweetheart roses, Gerber daisies, peonies, irises, arranged in a massive burst of color. The vase was so heavy I struggled to carry it.

As soon as I placed the flowers on my dining room table and took a photo, I texted Ezra.

"Whatever are you doing, you crazy man?" I scolded. "These are extraordinary!"

"Not as much as you, Peach. I love beautiful things, including flowers, and I wanted you to have these."

Ezra's work included frequent international travel. But without fail, a magnificent bouquet arrived on my doorstep every Friday for the next twelve weeks.

In the first month of our dating, he took a trip to London. One evening at dinner at his hotel, he asked the waiter to set an extra place for me. He sent me the photo of his meal and an empty plate with a full setup across from him.

"It makes me feel better to imagine you are here," he texted. Dining on oysters, he told me he would find a way to share his meal.

A week later, a small box arrived marked with international postage. Inside was an oyster shell with a message he had handwritten with a sharpie.

"Kiss me, Kate! You turn me on! Always, Ezra."

Was it to last? Could it last?

With weekend trips to the Tanglewood Music Festival in the Berkshire mountains, giant orchids sent to my office, gifts of artisan jewelry presented from a trip to Israel, tickets for my daughter and me to see *Hello, Dolly* on Broadway, and dinner with him after (and of course, the weekly bouquet), what was not to like?

"You are my source of energy, Peach. We need an extension cord to plug me in from your home to mine. Really, I have not felt the energy level I am feeling with you in many, many years, and the distance doesn't interfere here. Your energy travels through that distance. Please keep it so!"

Four months passed in the whirling dervish of a transcontinental relationship, and then Ezra invited me to spend a night at his house. I had only visited his home during the day, high on a hill in his quaint New Jersey town. When he had given me the tour, he had burned incense and muttered low incantations when we kissed in his sunroom, telling me the spirits were passing between us.

Even though we had been seeing a lot of each other between his trips and my work, spending the night at Ezra's home wasn't the direction I felt I should go. With the talk of animal spirits and energy flow, I didn't want to be captive there. So, I declined the overnight, agreeing to meet for dinner near his town.

By then, I knew that it was time. Time to say goodbye.

I had adored the adventure, the attention, the courting, the big dates, and the "nothing off-limits" approach.

But Ezra and I came from different worlds. And it would take one of us to say it.

When I arrived at the restaurant and met him inside, I told him I wanted to buy dinner. It was my way of feeling better about having a conversation that would end in concluding our relationship. He looked sheepish but agreed.

There was so much food we packed it up, so I could send leftovers home with him. I paid the check and asked if we could sit for a moment longer.

With a giant paper bag on the table between us, I told Ezra he was magnificent, but that I was wrong for him.

He smiled sadly and said:

"Guess what? I had planned tonight to tell you the same thing."

The evening ended with our parting under the streetlamp with one more kiss and one more giant bear hug. It was over. We were both sad.

I had gotten used to Ezra's magical way of courting. No more flowers, no more strawberries, no more chocolate cake. Even more, I appreciated and would miss his positive way of seeing the world.

The fire that he lit has stayed with me. As has the searching, hoping, and reaching for possibilities.

"Ask always . . . what's the point?" he was fond of saying. "Then go for it. The universe listens."

EARL the Engineer

♫ You Can't Hurry Love ♫

Artist: The Supremes

Meeting for an early dinner at the classic Dallas restaurant was Earl's idea. That he chose such an elegant spot was a good sign. I was back in Texas for a few days and pleased to join him at a place where I had enjoyed delicious and lengthy meals. We would have a real chance to get acquainted on a first date.

An old-moneyed, people watching establishment, Café Pacific is an anchor tenant in the exclusive Highland Park Village. Because of its location and excellent food, the fine dining fish house has been in favor with Dallas society for almost forty years.

Located in a premier corner of the historic high fashion shopping center, the restaurant looks swanky even on the outside. Dark green canopy awnings set off the beveled leaded glass front door. With an elegant interior decorated with mahogany woods, gold framed wall mirrors, and distinctive black and white patterned marble floors, the accoutrements spell exclusivity.

On the night Earl invited me to meet him, luxury cars queued up for valet parking ranged from a shiny black Bentley to a pristinely restored vintage white T-bird convertible. I didn't care that my black SUV rental was a "don't look at me" generic brand. A New Yorker now, I had nothing to prove. The attendant who took my car was friendly enough without being obsequious.

The evening was starting well enough.

But in my first year of dating after divorce, I had learned never to completely predict how an experience would go. I always kept an open mind, knowing there were at least four possible plot lines:

A) fabulous and exciting

B) enjoyable and interesting

C) tolerable but forgettable

D) downright awful

On the drive to meet Earl, I kept turning over in my mind several nagging thoughts. There was an overeagerness in his first text message, suggesting date scenario C—or even D—could be a possibility.

"I've just seen your profile, and if you are as lovely and sophisticated in person as you are in photos, I am a lucky man," he began.

"If you lived in Texas, I would camp on your doorstep! I would like to take you to dinner. I can arrange to be anywhere you wish on any evening you wish. I am so sure we would have a MOST interesting conversation."

We had connected a few days earlier as I flew into Texas. Earl had a typical profile with no red flags. Photos showed him in conventional business attire, a familiar look to me. The photo settings seemed innocuous enough, though not easily identifiable.

What I couldn't figure out was how old Earl was. Despite his good features, nicely styled brown hair, and professional look, I was suspicious the photos weren't current.

One clue was his changing hairline from image to image. And in the comparison of photo smiles, several looked forced, like grinning made his mouth hurt. And then in one shot, his stance seemed stiff and vaguely robotic, as if he could fall off balance leaning very far left or right.

We talked on the phone once. That was the final clue he might be older than he said. It was not only his slightly hesitant tone. He just sounded tired.

In the text banter leading up to the date, he defined his hopes for dating:

"I want a long-term relationship. I haven't yet found the woman I want to wake up to every morning."

Not intending to dissuade him from his hopes I could be "the one," but yet to point out the obvious, I answered back:

"You know I live in New York, right?"

"Yes, I know, but if there is chemistry, we could be on fire for each other. Nothing would stop me from getting to you. You just never know. Keep the faith."

Even as Earl expressed hopes that he could find an LTR (long-term relationship), he signaled a hint of anxiety about his eligibility.

Two days before we were to meet, Earl sent me a text at 3 AM:

"Have you given any thought to our age difference? I take good care of myself and get enough sleep and all. I am a clean eater too. Just wondering. Very excited to see you."

"Good to know about you," I responded with a non-answer the next day. "I have had enjoyable experiences meeting all types of people."

With no apologies for the early predawn text, Earl's next text communication landed during the day. He inquired about my exact arrival time for our date.

"Dinner is at 6. It was the only time the restaurant could get us in. And besides, I like to go to bed around the time the sun sets. I want to be there fifteen minutes before you . . . to get ready," he continued, mysteriously.

Trying to imagine what his pre-dinner early arrival ritual was (and curious why he even gave me a heads up he had one), I couldn't resist inquiring:

"Do tell!"

He answered with three emojis:

Red wine.

Red wine.

A kissy face.

Was he saying he needed two glasses of wine to fortify himself before meeting me? I could have fun with this, but I resisted the urge.

"I'll be there at 6, as planned," I said. "Don't know yet what I'll have on, but I'll find you. You'll be the one with the red wine!"

I had given little thought to what I would wear. This date was an unexpected addition to my calendar. Even though I always had a rule to dress appropriately for the weather and the setting, in this situation, I was limited to what was in my suitcase.

Luckily, I had packed for the Texas summer. Still 100 degrees in the shade in early September, Dallas was hot, hot, hot. The heat meant I could get away with summer clothes, just not white. (No self-respectable Dallas woman would ever wear white after Labor Day!)

I wasn't traveling with a wardrobe as chic as those of the restaurant's clientele. But I had packed a red sweater twin set with white piping, which I wore over an eye-catching gauze mosaic-patterned long skirt.

As I walked towards the door of the restaurant, I caught a glance of the hem of my skirt, skimming my new black pumps with their discreet snakeskin pattern on the heels. Even though they said 'Texas' more than 'New York', I had found them on sale while shopping with my daughter. Now I was glad I had them.

And I had another acceptable accessory. A small-check black and white dinner bag hung on my shoulder from an intertwined brass and leather chain. Discreet and understated, with a tassel that gently sashayed, I was confident it would be considered a verifiable Dallas look.

I pulled open the restaurant's heavy front door and immediately felt at home in the familiar setting. Well-heeled customers sat at white linen-draped tables, beautifully adorned with lush white floral bouquets in clear round vases. Each arrangement sparkled under perfectly spaced pin lights in the ceiling. Waitstaff, looking official and engaged, bustled between a small private dining room off the entrance and the elegant main dining room in the center.

Grateful I had been here before and knew the way, I nodded at the maître d' at the door, headed straight into the foyer, and then took a quick left into the bar. An inverted L shape, the room has three dining tables on the long axis and two small ones at the turn. All eight barstools were occupied for happy hour. Latecomers clustered around, fending for themselves, and hoping to catch the eye of a busy bartender.

I quickly surveyed the scene and immediately spotted Earl. He sat at a two-top table directly facing the entrance. He brightened when he saw me, as if relieved I was real and had shown up.

"We were just talking about you," he said eagerly, motioning to a female bartender standing near the table. "And it was good! And now it's SO much better that you are here."

Offering me a seat, he stood up and gave me an awkward, crushing hug, and then stepped back to look at me. "You're perfect!" he exclaimed. "Now, let's have a drink!"

It had taken me just a few seconds to realize that this evening (and this man) would not be an A or even a B. My instincts had been right.

He was eager. Too eager.

This was a C or D night. Time would tell.

I sat to Earl's right. Immediately, I spied a large grease spot on the right shoulder of his pale blue, ill-fitting sports coat. I could see it even more clearly when he leaned towards me and heaved his right arm over the back of my chair. The spot was a talisman for the evening.

True to his text emoji, Earl had started on red wine before I arrived. He rushed to ask what I wanted, handing me the wine menu. The wines were listed by classes. Pointing with an unsteady finger to the first class—the least expensive—he proudly showed me what he was drinking.

When I made my selection from that same grouping, Earl patted my hand. "Atta girl," he said. "I'll go get it."

Jumping up from the table, he jerkily ran the two or three steps to the bar. That gave me a few seconds to get a glance at him from a distance.

Slim and slight, Earl had the vibe of a country undertaker. His oversized jacket was of a pattern and material that screamed: "I am really trying hard to wear the right thing here."

Returning to the table with a slightly shaky gait, Earl looked glad to get back to his seat. He resettled quickly, again slinging his arm over the back of my chair.

"So, I am really glad to meet you. I want to really get to know you in the time we have. And I can already tell this is just the start of a magical journey. When is your next trip to Texas?"

If Earl picked up on my look of amused disbelief, he didn't let on. His next sentence was a clear indicator that my reaction to his opening statement had gone right over his head.

"Before you start telling me everything about you, tell me first when you think you'll have another trip to Texas. I have a four-bedroom house, and next time, I want you to stay with me."

“How kind,” I said. “But first, tell me about you.”

The floodgates opened. It was as if Earl hadn’t talked about his life in its entirety EVER. And worse, perhaps few had cared to ask.

Clearly unsure where to start, Earl began with his birth. He moved from describing his toddler years (what he could remember) to his childhood, and then on to his teenage years. When the pieces of his narrative didn’t connect or had big gaps, I’d nudge him back to the timeline.

Married twice, no kids, Earl’s career in industrial design had been satisfying. But it had ended disappointingly in a forced retirement he hadn’t quite figured out how to navigate. A recent romance was over too.

As Earl talked, what he shared was a recitation of facts without perspective. Even when he provided the details, he skimmed over any context.

He appeared to be a man alone—without a real support team, a network, or even a lifeline.

“So, who are your friends? How do you spend your time?” I prompted.

“I have a dog,” he answered. “Now let’s get dinner,” he changed the subject. “You can have anything you want. I am going to have an appetizer. I like the shrimp rem—oh—la—OOH—day. Ever had that? I’ll share.”

Scanning the menu and prices, which seemed almost modest next to New York City offerings, I searched for the most conservative choice.

“The iceberg wedge salad looks good to me,” I said.

With a visible sigh of relief, and a congratulatory backslap of my upper arm, he answered enthusiastically:

"Great choice! I'll have one too! I'll split my appetizer with you."

Before the shrimp remoulade and salads arrived, Earl took full advantage of our currently empty table to propel his body in my direction.

Throwing his right grease-stained shoulder and chest my way, he simultaneously lurched in, smiled, and tossed his arm on the back of my chair. Then, as if realizing maybe he'd invaded my personal space, he jerked back, removed his arm, and delivered another backhanded slap to my upper arm.

These 'advance it in/move it out' gyrations animated the continuing tales of Earl's life story. I assimilated very little of what he said, so preoccupied was I with trying to anticipate the pattern of his herky-jerky upper body foreplay.

Finally, several lifetimes later, the shrimp remoulade was served. Earl pulled the plate close to him, forcing me to lean towards him if I wanted a bite.

When my fork was poised mid-air, Earl asked inquisitively: "Are you a Christian?"

"Well, I grew up Catholic, as I mentioned, and my uncle was a priest. I don't practice now, but I think that qualifies me."

Earl looked almost joyful. Grabbing my left hand, which wasn't holding my fork, he announced:

"I am saying the blessing."

With his head bowed, and his chin practically grazing the tower of shrimp, Earl began:

"Dear God, thank you for bringing Kate and me together. This lovely creature was meant for me, and I pray that you find a way to get us going and keep us a couple. Lord, put on Kate's soul the joy of intersection with a godly man. Just to be clear, God, I am talking about me."

With that clarifying conclusion, Earl's head popped back up.

"Dig in," he beamed, as he inhaled a giant forkful of shrimp.

Still hoping to secure my first bite, I asked him to tell me about his dog. As if he had been waiting for that invitation all evening, he whipped out his phone.

"Look!" he showed me, pointing to a blurry image in a field of grass. "Isn't she magnificent? Her name is Clementine."

"Oh, yes," I said, not asking for more details. "I'm glad you have her."

"Just to be clear," Earl emphasized. "You'd have a higher ranking in my life than she would. In my last relationship, she slept in the bed. Maybe it was her chewing a bone all night that caused a problem. I don't know. But I've learned my lesson. With you, if you objected to the sleeping arrangement, we would go together to buy my Clementine a dog bed. I want to share everything with you."

Having snagged two small forkfuls of the appetizer for myself, I glanced at the plate and saw that only one bite of shrimp remoulade remained. "Mind if I have it?" he asked, pulling the plate even closer to him. "I have to keep my energy up for later."

The wedge salads were served next, and I was more than grateful to have my own plate. I watched as Earl sliced and diced his entire wedge into small bite-size pieces, creating a giant mound of broken lettuce and blue cheese, completely obliterating the chef's intended presentation.

Noting I didn't follow suit, he piped up. "Don't forget to chew real good. If one of those hunks of bacon gets stuck in your throat, I don't want to have to do the Heimlich."

Lucky for me, I consumed my salad without catastrophe. Not so lucky for Earl. Even with the bite-size preparation, he managed to drop not one, but three fork drippings of dressing onto his lap. I didn't want to imagine the location of *those* grease spots.

When the waiter removed our plates and asked about orders of entrees, dessert or coffee, Earl quickly said: "Oh, no, she doesn't want any." I smiled pleasantly as the waiter nodded in my direction.

"It's been a lovely evening, Earl," I said. "The food was really delicious."

Thankfully, the bill came within minutes. Earl got out reading glasses to peruse every line. Running his hand down the page, he underlined each entry with his finger as if he were a first grader learning how to read. Finally, resigned to the numbers, he placed his credit card in the leather holder.

"You know what would be fun next time? Maybe we can have a picnic. It stays hot here in Texas for a long time. I bet you are a good cook. Do you know how to make potato salad?"

"If you'll excuse me," I said. "I'll answer that in a moment."

I walked swiftly out of the bar, and across the dining room to the ladies' room. Parting the heavy red velvet drapes that framed the door, I pushed my way inside and took a moment to catch my breath.

Then I smiled. This was already a night to remember. What were the chances I would have an evening like this in any other place but Texas?

When I returned through the dining area to the bar, I saw that our table was unoccupied. Momentarily wondering whether Earl had slipped out and walked the check, I feared even more that he was lurking in a dark corner, ready to throw an arm over my shoulder.

But I found him outside, handing the valet parker his ticket. I handed over my own.

"Oh, let me take care of this," Earl said, getting out a money clip.

"Well, darn it," he shucked. "Seems I don't have any change here. We'll be back though, and I can cover it next time."

I pulled out a ten and handed it to the valet.

Sidling right up next to me as we waited for the cars, Earl gushed: "I don't know when I've had a better evening. I hope you felt the same. I can't wait to see you again!"

A small mercy, Earl's car arrived first, and he sprinted awkwardly to the driver's side. Waving and blowing kisses, he hopped in.

Not long after getting back to my hotel, I received a text from Earl:

"You were a lovely surprise. Rare when a person looks better than their picture, but you do. I enjoyed our honest conversation. Interesting how many things we have in common. Next time you come back to Dallas, stay with me. I'll introduce you to Clementine, and you can introduce me to your potato salad."

To which I sent back three emojis:

A dog.

Red wine.

A picnic basket.

Hope springs eternal.

STEFAN the Scholar

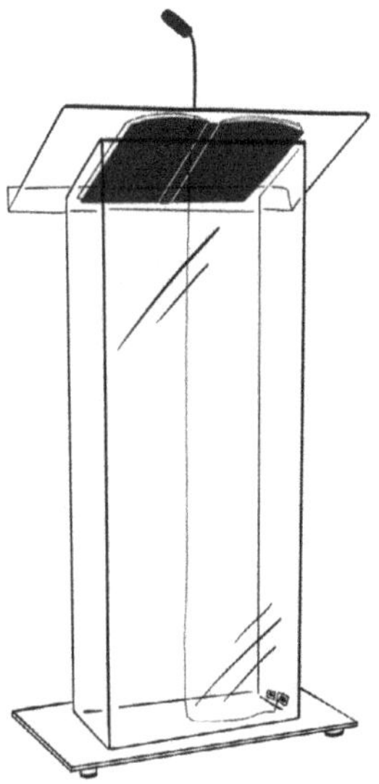

♫ R-E-S-P-E-C-T ♫

Artist: Aretha Franklin

I was not supposed to be there. The three-day conference was for members only. Over 2,000 people attended the annual meeting, held in alternating big cities in the U.S. and Canada. This summer it was in New York City.

Lucky for me, my longtime friend Laura was the organizer and program planner, and she worked her magic to secure me a VIP guest pass.

The location was the flagship Marriott Marquis hotel in Times Square. With 48 stories, 1949 rooms, and 125,000 square feet, the convention-sized facility is a small city. Organized around an atrium lobby, multiple ballrooms, exhibition halls, restaurants, and sleeping rooms, the Marriott Marquis is the only hotel in New York City with a revolving rooftop restaurant. Accommodating hundreds of thousands of guests each year, everything about the hotel feels big.

The larger-than-life setting was ideal for the conference. Beyond thrilled to be in the audience for a lineup of stellar business speakers, including a past mayor of New York City, I planned to take advantage of this singular chance to meet movers and shakers in my new home of Manhattan.

The conference started on Sunday. Arriving early on the sticky overcast morning in July, I was proud of myself for navigating the subway system to the correct station. For the unpredictable summer weather forecast, I carried an umbrella in case I encountered a downpour walking through Times Square. Gambling it was the right choice,

I wore a sleeveless black and green dress, cropped black blazer with three-quarter-length sleeves, and a conservative pair of black heels.

Standing in line at registration, I sized up the crowd. A distinguished group of business-attired executives chatted amiably, many seeming to have longstanding connections and relationships.

That's okay, I told myself. Just act like you belong.

Once officially registered, I proudly donned my plastic-sheathed conference nametag, dangling from a red silk lanyard cord. In large letters, my name "KATE SOMERSET" appeared on the top line. "VIP Guest" in slightly smaller letters was on the line below. At least, the placard was invitingly vague.

Hoping to avoid early conversations about what a VIP guest was, I slipped past the large crowd gathered in the foyer of the giant ballroom and made my way inside.

What a room! Eight shimmering crystal chandeliers hung from a 30-foot-tall ceiling. The giant stage at the far end of the room was flanked by two enormous projection screens. The artistically lit acrylic podiums on stage left and stage right underscored the serious nature of the event.

Hundreds of participants were beginning to mill into the ballroom to take their seats. I had no group, and I knew no one.

Squaring my shoulders back, I walked all the way to the front of the room and chose an aisle seat on the third row. Stowing my bag underneath the dark leather padded conference chair, I settled in. Looking up, I hadn't realized how close my seat was to the podium on stage left. I would have a great view.

Opening the glossy conference program book, I began studying. Within seconds, I spotted the photograph. A shockingly handsome man's headshot and bio appeared next to the time of a mid-afternoon plenary session. The speaker's topic was how to be memorable in building brand loyalty.

I circled the entry. This presentation would be right up my alley. I needed to build my brand. And even if I learned nothing, I knew I would relish watching such an attractive speaker. His first name was Stefan. I could remember that.

The morning flew by. Presenters were prepared, engaging, and covered challenging subject matter, each more fascinating than the one before. At the noon break, I found my friend and thanked her for securing the ticket.

"You are welcome," Laura said. "I want you to get as much out of this as possible. Go to the exhibit hall after the business luncheon. There are a number of people you should meet. I'll stop by to introduce you."

As soon as the speeches at lunch ended, I headed to the exhibit hall two floors down. The space was buzzing.

Conference attendees gathered round the multiple exhibit booths, each set up with professional signage, lighting, and pipe and drape formality. Attention-grabbing displays were staffed by gregarious representatives of the companies that were exhibiting. They served as conference barkers, exhorting the crowd to look their way. A crush of participants, enjoying free refreshments, clustered in animated conversation groups.

Glancing at my watch, I had thirty minutes before Stefan's session began.

Laura waved from across the room, beckoning me over to a large crowd. Even before I had spoken to each of them, I was out of time.

Escaping from the exhibit hall like a teenager trying to sneak home after curfew, I sprinted up two sets of escalators, three steps at a time. At the turn to the second escalator, one of my heels flew off, stranded below me as I kept riding up.

I yelled at a stranger to throw it back. Barely missing the top of my head, the shoe sailed above me. I was able to catch up to it just seconds before it got stuck in the gears of the escalator.

Sliding my foot into the heel, I ran for the massive doors of the ballroom. All were closed.

I heard applause in the ballroom. Oh, no! I was late.

A presenter was introducing Stefan, who already stood by the podium at stage left. The chair I had sat in during the morning sessions was just three rows in front of him, with all my conference materials stuffed underneath.

I had no choice but to go there.

Praying that the seat was unoccupied, I walked the long gauntlet back to the front. I could feel the heat of hundreds of pairs of eyes staring at me. I didn't engage.

And YES! My chair was empty.

And YES! Stefan was more strikingly attractive in the flesh than any still photo could capture.

I reclaimed my seat and pulled a legal pad out of my bag. Wishing I knew stenography to keep up with the lightning-fast presentation, I scribbled five pages of single-spaced notes. Stefan was provocative, insightful, and funny. When he finished, I knew I had to meet him.

I wasn't the only one who had that thought.

As Stefan left the stage, he walked away from the podium in front of me and down into the waiting crowd on the opposite side of the ballroom. Even from where I stood, it wasn't hard to see the long queue of fans who wanted to shake his hand. With a fast-footed dash to the other side of the room, my frantic speed only earned me a spot dead last in line.

In what seemed like forever, Stefan's admirers inched forward. Now it was a race—could he speak to everyone before he was ushered away to clear the room for the next presentation?

I did the math. Thirty minutes until the next speaker. At least twenty people were ahead of me. It was a gamble.

While I waited, I rehearsed my opening line. Stefan had shared strategies of successful companies that build customer loyalty. The research showed it wasn't enough to have a recognizable brand. Companies must over-deliver, giving customers something extra they didn't expect.

What could I do with that?

What would I say to make myself memorable?

My reveries kept me occupied as I steadily worked my way to second in line. The man ahead of me had Stefan's ear, telling stories about a mutual friend who had attended Stefan's Ivy League alma mater. They nodded together like old pals who shared a secret joke. This could go on forever.

Even worse for me . . . how could Stefan switch gears to talk to a stranger who had no idea how to begin the conversation? Just as I stepped forward to say hello, a conference organizer walked between us. "You don't have to take this one," he said. "We are out of time."

Undeterred, I looked past him and caught Stefan's eye. He looked back.

"Let me talk to her," he insisted, taking me by the arm, and moving me away from the crowd.

"Hi," Stefan began, looking through me with piercing deep blue eyes. Very tall and trim, he wore a European-cut suit perfectly. His sartorial style was conservative professorial with an edge. His thick wavy brown hair framed a high-browed patrician forehead.

Stefan's demeanor towards me was simultaneously serious and interested.

"Your presentation was one of the most captivating I have ever heard," I began. "Your research and how you related it to the audience was masterful. And the way you wove in the humor was perfect."

Looking genuinely pleased, he responded: "That's high praise. Thank you, sincerely."

"There is one thing," I went on, "that I believe you left out. If you decide in the future to talk about it, you could have the audience eating out of the palm of your hand."

Cocking his head to the side, Stefan seemed both confused and amused.

"Yes . . .", he said.

"The one topic you didn't bring up is how to build trust and loyalty in online dating. Take it from me." I fixed my gaze on his eyes. "If you could shine a light on this subject, you'd help millions."

"Oh," he answered, "and are you an expert?"

"Well," I said, with more assurance than I felt. "I am newly single, living in New York, and have been out with men I have met online. So yes, that makes me an expert. Here's my business card, which mentions nothing about this expertise. But let me assure you, the opportunity for research is ripe."

Smiling, Stefan took the card, and looked carefully at my name. As he extended his hand to shake mine, he said: "Well, Kate, this will go down in history as the only time anyone has offered this unique evaluation of my presentation. I'll take your advice to heart."

My own heart was palpitating as I stepped away. Was he flirting with me? Even a little? Yes, I was DEFINITELY flirting with him. I made a beeline across the ballroom for Laura, my friend.

"Laura," I gasped, catching up with her. "A quick question—is Stefan single?"

Laura, who was both cautious and discreet, arched her eyebrows and answered:

"I wouldn't have any idea about his personal life. I just book these speakers, you know, not inquire about their marital status." Looking sternly at me, she went on: "What have you gone and done now?" I told her what happened.

"Really," she said. "I will be interested to see what comes of this."

"You're not the only one!" I replied.

After the roller-coaster day, and back in my neighborhood, I decided to take myself out for an alfresco dinner at a charming Italian bistro. The rain clouds had disappeared and the sultry air cooled at twilight. My jacket now felt comforting instead of suffocating. The Italian waitstaff at Bottega fluttered around, bringing bread, water, and announcing the specials.

"I'll have a glass of your best red wine," I said. "I am celebrating."

I planned to send Stefan an email in a couple of days once the conference ended. The excellent house cabernet made it easier to imagine how I was going to construct the message. It wasn't enough to be complimentary. I needed a call to action to motivate him to answer.

The next morning, I was back at the conference, but mentally miles away. The keynote speaker was former New York City Mayor Michael Bloomberg. It was a privilege to hear him talk about his commitment to philanthropy. Even though the talk was inspiring, I had Stefan on my mind.

Lost in thought, my phone vibrated with a notification. I quickly glanced down at my lap. My email inbox had a new message. I couldn't see the entire content without opening the email. But the first few lines made my heart race.

> Hi, Kate,
>
> It was great meeting you yesterday. I'm glad we had the chance to talk but am sorry we didn't have more time.

Wow . . . I couldn't wait for Mayor Bloomberg to end his speech so I could read Stefan's full message. A torturous 45 minutes later, during rapturous applause and a standing ovation, I had that window.

Stefan's email continued:

> Maybe the next time I am in NYC, I can take you to lunch or dinner, and you can share your online dating stories with me. I am certain you receive much more attention than most women, so I would love to hear about all the ways men have gone about meeting you! I'm sure they will make me laugh or leave me shocked, but all will be interesting (and maybe I will learn something.)
>
> I hope you enjoy the rest of the conference and make some great connections.
>
> Take care, Kate.
>
> Stefan

Had this really happened? Did he intend to stay in touch? Was the meeting he proposed a date, or was it more likely he was just being friendly? Not knowing how to interpret the message, I wasted no time in replying.

> Hi, Stefan,
>
> How terrific to hear from you! I couldn't stop thinking last night about your presentation, and all the ways it impacted me. Your remarks were relevant to so many aspects of my life and work, that I wanted to pull you aside for a one-on-one.
>
> So yes, I would enjoy a longer time to talk with you. We can discuss online dating, and I can show you the art (not the science) of how the confounded system works. Maybe together we can create a new one! The world needs it.
>
> Congratulations again on a fabulous presentation. Seriously, in all the conferences and sessions I've attended, yours was one of the very, very best.
>
> How often are you in NYC? Hope to see you again soon.
>
> Kate
>
> PS Since you shared facts about your life with the conference audience, I'll return the favor. Here are mine: I am an Irish Catholic, I eat French fries, my favorite dessert is apple pie, I grew up in the South, I am the oldest of three, and my Myers Briggs score is ENTJ.

Two hours later, Stefan answered back:

> I would love to hear more about all of your past adventures and the ones still in front of you. I promise I will make good on meeting you for lunch or dinner (your choice)—especially now that I know that French fries and apple pie are all you need!

> I am on my way to Maui for an event on Wednesday, and from there to Jakarta for another on Saturday (quite the glamorous life, huh? More time on an airplane than on the ground!) So, I will let you know what my schedule is like when I get back. Thanks for sharing a few facts about your life with me.
> I'm sure the things you mentioned don't even begin to scratch the surface, so I look forward to discovering what you left out.

Using all the restraint I could muster, I waited four long hours before responding. During that time, my brain at the conference was on autopilot. All I could think about were three things:

1) An internationally known speaker was certifiably intent on talking with me again.

2) Stefan had initiated the conversation, and so soon. AND,

3) Our communication was likely not going to be all business!

I answered back:

> Stefan,
> Only you might be able to make me trust that eating French fries and apple pie in the same meal is a good plan. Given that we have both put items on the table for discussion, let's plan to have dinner. Safe travels as
> you wow audiences around the world. I can't wait
> to hear all about it.
> Kate

Twelve days went by . . . and nothing. Even though Stefan was traveling, there was no guarantee he wouldn't forget all about our conference communication. He hadn't told me when he was coming back to New York. And we had made no plans. The ball was still in my court.

Thinking carefully about the time of day, and the day of the week to send an email, I wrote a new message at 4:30 PM on a Friday.

Stefan's workweek was probably over, and perhaps he might glance at my email at an airport.

> RE: Maui, Jakarta, and Parts Unknown
>
> Hi, Stefan,
>
> You have successfully avoided the erratic weather the Northeast is having. My umbrella needs to go in the shop!
>
> I am now keeping a diary for you of online dating techniques, profiles, and experiences. It's not very thick since it's relatively new to me, but at least it's entertaining!
>
> Have a great weekend,
>
> Kate

In 39 minutes, Stefan answered.

> Hello, Kate. What a nice surprise! I am still wandering the planet, although this week, it is in far less interesting (and beautiful) places than last week.
>
> I will be in NYC on Thursday. If you are free and would like to have dinner that evening, I would love to hear your stories!
>
> If not, please keep adding to the diary and we can go over it another time.
>
> Thanks for emailing me, Kate. Enjoy the rest of your weekend and let me know about Thursday.
>
> Stefan

Now my mind was racing.

He answered. We had a date. What if I hadn't emailed him?

Would he have taken the lead? Was he married? In a relationship? Interested at all in me . . . or only in my dating stories? First, I had to accept the invitation. My answer should indicate interest without appearing as excited as I really was.

> Hi, Stefan,
>
> Thank you for the opportunity to have dinner. Yes, amazingly Thursday is great. Scheduling around work always seems to be my Achilles' heel. So, I am thrilled this opportunity matched with your travels.
>
> Since I have seven email accounts, let's try texting. Here's my cell. I'll look forward to seeing you.
>
> Travel safely,
>
> Kate

Stefan sent a quick reply:

> Great, Kate. I'll give you more details next week. Coming back to NYC will be far more appealing since I know you are there. Have a good weekend.

It was six days until our dinner.

As comfortable (to a point) as I had become in meeting strangers on first dates, this felt different. Stefan and I had spoken in person for one minute in a room of 2,000 people. I knew very little about him, and he about me.

Even more daunting, he didn't live in my city. I didn't know where he lived. His website provided no information on his hometown. Stefan was a celebrity of sorts. Yes, the stakes were definitely higher. He was a citizen of the world.

For the first time in years, I laid out outfit options and took photos of them. A navy dress, all business? Pink for Texas? Maybe not a dress—what about a black and white fitted top with black pants? Or how about all white for impact?

I texted photos to both female and male friends seeking advice. The answers came back. No one was in agreement:

> The first one is sophisticated.
>
> This one says all business.
>
> That choice is playful.
>
> This one is sexy.
>
> Maybe this one is too serious.

I was even more confused than if I had never asked.

Trusting my intuition, I chose a white pique summer dress with an off-the-shoulder capped sleeve and a ruched waist. A black sweater for my bare shoulders, and black peep toe heels no doubt sent a mixed message, which was akin to exactly how I was feeling. A little like work, a little like a date. Who knew how this was going to go?

We were meeting at the Sea Fire Grill, a fine-dining seafood restaurant in Midtown. I arrived early to beat Stefan. I wanted the advantage of watching him walk in, so I could at least pretend to myself I was relaxed and collected.

Thwarting my plan, the long and narrow interior of the restaurant had poor sight lines. Stepping inside from the street, patrons walk straight into the bar, and then from there into the dining area. The railroaded entry meant there was nowhere for me to comfortably wait with my eye on the entrance. Opting not to sit at the actual bar with my back to the door, I chose a mirrored cocktail deuce across from it.

Stefan was due in fifteen minutes. I had an unobstructed view of the street from the cocktail table. But a giant mirrored column next to me blocked any view of the restaurant's front door.

When a waiter offered me a drink menu, I asked only for ice water. Every time I took a nervous sip, condensation from the glass dripped onto the mirrored tabletop and then cascaded onto my lap and legs.

The suspense was killing me, and my dress was getting soaked.

I had been waiting for twenty minutes. He was officially late. Maybe he wasn't coming after all. We had not exchanged texts that day. Perhaps the joke was on me.

And then boom! Stefan's suited profile appeared through the window across the bar. He was on the sidewalk outside. His gait was almost a gallop, his long legs in an urgent forward stride. Then just as quickly, he was gone.

Did I dream I had seen him? No. In the time it took me to glance away from the window and back to the room, Stefan was standing right in front of me. He wiped his wavy hair away from his brow and gave me a flustered grin.

"Hi," he said, as we both reached forward for a quick, but electric hug.

"Please excuse me for a moment," he said.

I stood up, and then as quickly sat back down, brushing more water off my lap. I barely had time to still my heartbeat, and he was back.

All I could think to say was: "Boy, that was quick!" Completely cringeworthy. I bit my tongue silently, wishing I could take back what had just come out of my mouth.

"Sorry to be so unsettled," he said. "My taxi had no air conditioning, then broke down six blocks from here. Rather than take the time to hail another one, I ran the rest of the way. My apologies for being late. But now I am here and happy to see you. Let's have dinner," he continued more calmly, and led me by the arm to the dining room.

The setting was perfect. Romantic and dark, our corner table gave us a panoramic view of the room. But my eyes were on Stefan, and his were on me.

The waiter broke the spell when he approached our table with menus. Stefan grinned at me, and then at our waiter, and announced: "The lady will have an order of French fries."

"Very good, sir," said the waiter, registering no surprise.

Within minutes, a giant bowl of Pommes Frites arrived. Stefan instructed the waiter to put them in front of me.

Sitting to Stefan's right, I leaned in, ignoring the delicious looking fries for the moment.

"I have a million questions," I said. "But before we get started, I must ask you something."

Taken aback at my serious tone, he responded: "Shoot!"

"I know so little about you, and look forward to finding out more," I said. "But first, tell me. Are you married?"

Looking completely shocked, Stefan responded. "What? Did you think I invited you to dinner as a trick? No, I am not married. I have been single for a very, very long time. In fact, you are the first date I have had in 25 years. That is, if we want to call tonight a date."

And so, began a night less about eating, and more about talking.

We ordered food we barely touched (even the Pommes Frites got cold). It was difficult to eat when neither of us looked down at our plates. We covered a gamut of topics from his life and work, to my life and move to New York, to online dating, and to Stefan's feeling he could never really be in a relationship.

"I lead a gypsy life," he explained. "I am a loner and don't want the obligations that go with dating and being responsible for another person's happiness. I find you intriguing, but I can't imagine doing what you do, putting yourself out there to meet new people night after night. Telling your story, hearing theirs. I admire you, and I wish I could be you, but I can't."

Despite his protestations, Stefan was completely engaged in our conversation. I could see it in his eyes. His arm brushed mine as we gestured and laughed and told stories. When his hand touched mine, he took it and didn't let it go.

We had been seated at 7:15. The restaurant was full. When I looked into the room again, the crowded restaurant was empty. Where had the night gone?

Closing time was 10 PM; they let us stay until 11.

When we finally stepped outside, Stefan gave me a long kiss, standing on the sidewalk, just as the restaurant staff turned off the exterior lights.

"Convenient," he laughed, cupping my face in his hands.

"I have to tell you something. You have been the first person I have been deeply interested in during the last two-and-a-half decades. I stayed in New York City tonight just to have dinner with you. I am now driving three hours back home, fueled by the adrenaline rush of tonight. You should consider that a real compliment. I really never do this. But I am glad I did."

He touched my face again and pulled me towards him.

"I had forgotten how wonderful this could be," he said, tenderly. "But I am exactly the wrong person for you," he sighed. "I would just hold you back. You are going to have a big life in New York. I can just tell. Don't let me keep you from it, 'Miss Katie'. I would never forgive myself."

And so, it ended, almost as quickly as it had begun.

On the first anniversary of our dinner, Stefan texted:

"Enjoying any French fries without me, Katie? Hoping your French fry addiction is alive and well. You know you didn't eat the ones I bought you."

"Oh, Stefan," I countered. "You allowed me to be a slimmer, better person that night. One could now conclude my French fry consumption is well under control, thanks to you.

It's a delight to remember where I was a year ago tonight . . . wondering what to wear to meet you. Even though I never finished the fries, that dinner (yes it was a date!) gave me a window into the Stefan who isn't on stage. And for that revelation and your honesty, I will always be grateful."

To which he replied:

"I told you things that night I had never spoken of before and won't again. I will never forget how respectful you were of my secrets. I will be grateful for the NEXT twenty-five years for that rare moment I had with you."

I haven't been back to the Sea Fire Grill. But now, every time I see Pommes Frites on a menu, I look around to see if Stefan is there.

NICK the Neighbor

♪♪ You've Got a Friend ♪♪

Artist: Carole King

When I moved into a Manhattan apartment building, I had been warned that living vertically with so many strangers would be a challenge. Preferring to see it as a grand adventure, I relished the opportunity to meet many new people—all in one place and each of us with the same address. Surely new friends were just around the corner.

There were so many shared experiences of living in a big building:

Being greeted by uniformed doormen, wearing cap and gloves, standing at the ready to launch the revolving door at the entrance.

Retrieving mail from the rows of brass bank-sized lock boxes in the mailroom.

Walking downstairs to the package corridor to retrieve Amazon shipments, where porters searched the stacks of daily deliveries for ones marked in black Sharpie with each apartment number.

Doing laundry in a room with 48 washers and dryers, and being right on time to retrieve your wash, to prevent another impatient resident from removing your things and tossing them in a wet clump on the long folding tables.

Running for one of the three busy elevators and squeezing into a packed car for the ride to one of 30 plus floors, all exact look-alikes.

Carrying heavy bags of groceries from the neighborhood market and making it to the apartment door without dropping one.

Walking the hall on your floor at mealtime and being hit with the strong smell of someone else's cooking.

Maintaining an even, disinterested expression with everyone you meet.

The last was the least easy to get used to. I was far too curious.

Who lives behind all those closed doors? What do they do? Would I enjoy getting to know them? Who will I run into in my hallway today?

Given the total number of apartments in my building, there were theoretically 750 people I needed to meet!

As I got accustomed to my new environment, I quickly learned my building's inhabitants welcomed newcomers with varying degrees of enthusiasm. Most of the interactions happened getting on, riding, and getting off the elevators. Rarely did people strike up a conversation in the common areas of the building.

Think of your building like a hotel, I was told, where people want their privacy. Even though residents don't hang a 'do not disturb' sign on their doors, pretend you can see it. Their apartment is their home. The only thing you share is a common hallway.

Don't engage.

Don't introduce yourself.

Keep your distance.

This approach both intrigued and horrified me. How could I live so close to so many people without getting to know ANYONE?

When I first moved into the building, I made an offer to the leasing manager.

"I would be delighted to organize an event for all single residents," I said brightly.

With uplifted eyebrows over his wire-rim glasses, Isaac looked at me.

"An emphatic no," he responded after a few minutes. "First, we've never had anybody make this suggestion. We couldn't tell you who the singles are," he said stiffly. "Above all else, we respect the privacy of our tenants. And second, we don't want the liability. What if a bad actor stalked you? And because you both lived in the same place, you could never get away from him. It could be drama," he warned. "And trust me, you don't want New York City drama."

Before I moved into the building, I had gotten similar advice from friends who were seasoned Manhattan dwellers.

Don't date anyone in your building!

Yes, it could seem romantic at first, but what if you run into each other at not-so optimum times—unpresentable in the laundry room or walking into the lobby disheveled from the weather.

Or what if you liked each other at first, but then the relationship got uncomfortable or fizzled? Heaven forbid you see him with another woman. It was all too messy, too awkward.

And because so many people live in your building, you'll never encounter the same person twice. It's just too much work to make a connection where you live. Go online and forget about it!

Undaunted, I made a vow to remain open to all opportunities. And I did.

A week after I moved in, there was a development. My new yoga teacher, a young raven-haired beauty who had been on a season of *The Bachelor,* was riding the elevator from the lobby to my apartment for our session.

Just as the doors were closing, a man squeezed in to join her. She pushed the button to the 18th floor. "Oh, that's where I am going!" he said in a friendly way. "Hi, I'm Nick. I'm new to the building. How do you like it here?"

"Oh, I am not a resident," Abby said. "I'm going to see a client."

"Well, have a good day," he responded as he exited, heading straight for the apartment across from the elevator.

Abby raced to my apartment, two doors away.

"I think I met a guy for you in the elevator! He's really cute and very friendly!"

I peppered her with questions:

"What's his full name?"

"I don't know. He only told me his first name—Nick."

"Describe his looks."

"Clean cut, nice smile, businessman type."

"How old is he?"

"I am not sure. I can't tell about middle-aged people. Definitely more your age than mine. But handsome for his age."

"Was he asking you out?"

"No, I just think he was trying to make a friend."

"Where does he live?"

"I know his apartment number, 18C!"

The wheels started turning. How could I meet Nick? It would take forever to run into him at the elevator. I didn't have his last name, so I couldn't find him on social media if he even had a presence there. I knew the building wouldn't tell me who he was. Heck, I didn't even know if he was single. But I had to figure this out.

Several days went by, and I hatched a plot. It was early summer when all Manhattan buildings do much-needed maintenance and renovations while the weather is good.

Each Friday, the building superintendent distributed paper

notices about the next week's construction and repair schedule. The rolled flyers were delivered to every door and placed between each door handle and door frame.

Since I saw Nick's door whenever I rode the elevator, I noticed his paper flyer had not moved on Friday. It was still there on Saturday. And on Sunday morning.

By Sunday afternoon, I decided to act. Walking nonchalantly from my apartment to his, I grabbed the notice from his door and hurried back to my apartment.

In my kitchen, I took a pen and scribbled an angled note on the paper:

> Hi, Nick. I'm your neighbor Kate in 18A. My yoga teacher met you in the elevator this week. She said you were new to the building. Me too! I'd be happy to tell you the ropes so far. If you're interested, let's have a drink. Here's my phone number. Feel free to text me or give me a call. Hope you're having a great weekend!

I carefully re-rolled the paper, walked down the hall to Nick's door, and stuck it back into the door handle.

Later Sunday night returning to my floor from collecting mail downstairs, I noticed the paper was gone.

Two days passed. I was checking out at CVS when a call from an unfamiliar area code popped up on my phone. I took a chance that it wasn't a Robocall, and answered it.

"Hi, Kate, this is Nick. I got your note on Sunday night when I returned from a business trip. It was really nice of you to reach out," he began. "And I would love to get together. How about this weekend for a drink or brunch? You pick the place. I don't know the neighborhood yet."

Nick sounded great on the phone. Warm, friendly, maybe a little cautious, but still open.

Recently divorced, he had moved into the building the week before he ran into Abby. A work promotion provided the opportunity to come to New York City from California. Like me, he had made a huge life transition, both in his work and personal life. He had two children in their 20s. I had a daughter around the same age.

There would be a lot to talk about.

We made plans for brunch on Saturday. "I'll meet you in the hall by the elevator," he said.

"Sure!" I answered, as we ended the call. "It'll be great to meet a new friend."

I followed up our phone call with a text:

> Hi, Nick,
>
> Thanks for the call! Great to talk to a neighbor.
>
> By the way, I didn't tell you, but my last name is Somerset.
>
> I frequently post on social media for my Texas friends. So, you'll find me there . . . Or in the trash room on our floor, dumping my recycling at 1 AM!
>
> Seriously, it will be fun to say hello in person this weekend!
>
> Looking forward to it.

Nick answered quickly:

> Yes, I agree it's nice to meet a neighbor. See you Saturday. Just knock on my door when you're ready.

Having Nick on the floor meant that now our shared hallway was not an anonymous space. And it never would be again, so long as we were neighbors, with one apartment in between.

For the rest of the week, I wondered what he looked like. And I tried to imagine how our conversation would go.

As importantly, I pondered how to dress for an 'I'm just meeting you for the first time as friends, and maybe there will be something more' weekend brunch.

On Saturday at 12:30 PM, I walked out of my door wearing skinny jeans, a white blouse, and cork wedge sandals accessorized with a red bracelet and earrings. A pop of color always helps, I thought, especially for a Texan in New York.

Waiting for me at the elevator was an attractive man, at least three inches taller than I was in my carefully chosen shoes. Abby had described him well—ruddy-cheeked, with friendly blue eyes, and a welcoming smile.

"I didn't even get the chance to knock on your door," I said.

"Next time," he answered, giving me a quick, easy hug. He didn't take his eyes off of me in the elevator.

Uva, the restaurant I suggested, was about six blocks away from our building, and the day was lovely. It was a quick walk, and our conversation on the way was fun.

Sitting outside at a high-top table on the restaurant's patio, we talked for two hours. Being with Nick was easy. The captivating twinkle in his eyes, and his quick and light-hearted laugh, enhanced our comfortable banter. He was a good listener too. It felt like we were old friends.

Because his divorce had been so recent, Nick volunteered he wasn't quite ready to date, answering the question I hadn't asked.

"I understand completely," I said reassuringly. "I'm only a few months ahead of you in being divorced. So, when you're ready, and if you want some reflections about how to start with online dating sites, I'm your girl."

He flashed a genuine smile and said: "I'll be sure to ask your advice when the time is right. And in the meantime, it's great to know you. Since I don't cook, I go out for dinner almost every night. I would love for you to join me anytime."

"Great!" I said, meaning it, asking myself whether I felt any chemistry, and wondering if he did.

When the check was finally presented, I put my hand on the leather sleeve.

"I'll buy your lunch if you buy mine," I winked.

Nick looked relieved. Going Dutch easily removed any stigma of what might've felt like a date. A pleasant, laid-back visit between two new neighbors removed any threat.

Nick waited for me as I stepped into the ladies' room. When I rejoined him, he was in a spirited conversation with a dog walker. A tiny older woman, she was trying to control seven dogs on individual leashes. As they pulled and tugged, eager to get moving, she planted her feet so as not to topple over, and fixed her gaze on him.

Then she looked from Nick to me, and back again, saying in his direction: "Oh, she's adorable! How long have you two been together?"

I felt the blood rise in my cheeks and glanced at him to see what he would do. "Oh, about three hours," he said, smiling. "We live in the same building!"

"Ah," said the dog walker. "The better to see each other!"

Nick and I gave each other amused looks and started the walk back to our building. As we crossed the street to enter the building's driveway, I pointed overhead. "Look at that odd scaffolding at the top. What kind of maintenance work could that be?" I asked him.

"I don't know," he said, gazing upward. "Let's go in and find out together."

Standing on duty at the revolving front door, Jesse, the doorman, had a singular reputation for getting into other people's business.

Nick approached him. "Hi, Jesse! Kate and I wondered . . ." He began when Jesse abruptly stopped him. "WAIT! How long has THIS been going on?!" Jesse asked, while looking intently at both of us.

"We just met today," Nick said. To which Jesse responded, "Nice. NICE!"

And then he gave Nick a high five. My cheeks turned crimson for the second time in 20 minutes.

Whatever the explanation for why the scaffolding was sticking out at a weird angle, I didn't hear it. I was preoccupied wondering what Nick thought about the not-so-subtle comment from Jesse.

When we got off the elevator on the 18th floor, Nick casually asked if I wanted to see his apartment. "I am still in boxes," he apologized. "I have been working so much I don't know when I'll ever get organized. But you may enjoy a look at the layout of a unit that's different from yours, since we were comparing notes about our space at lunch."

"Sure, I would love to," I said. "It will be the first apartment besides my own in the building I have gotten to tour."

After the brief walk through of Nick's apartment, I invited him to see mine. Back in the hall, we passed apartment 18B and arrived at my door.

"Wow!" he exclaimed, as we walked in. "You look like you have been settled here forever."

"Not really," I demurred. "I am not going to show you the closets!"

He laughed and turned to say goodbye. "This was great!" he said enthusiastically. "Have a good weekend."

An hour later, I sent him a message:

> Hi, Nick, I loved meeting you. Thought you would enjoy seeing some 'what not to do' photos posted by men I swiped left on. I am happy to help you succeed at this online dating adventure when you are ready.

A few minutes later, he responded:

> I enjoyed meeting you too. Thanks for getting in touch. I'll definitely look forward to sharing dating stories when the time is right.

After our first meeting, I ran into Nick leaving or entering the building, or coming and going in the laundry room, or recycling his trash at the same time I did late at night. Before our lunch, I never saw him. Now I was bumping into him all the time.

Whenever we saw each other, Nick was always friendly, stopping to talk, and asking questions about what I was up to. At the end of each conversation, we exchanged wishes for a great evening or a good weekend.

Two weeks later, I had Friday night plans to go to Rao's, an "impossible to get into" Manhattan restaurant. It had taken months for my friends Norm and Myra from Los Angeles to snag the table. They were flying to New York in time to dine at the famous Italian eatery. I was lucky to be included in their party of four.

In late afternoon, the other member of our party dropped out because she wasn't feeling well. That left one highly coveted seat empty for dinner that night.

Since Norm and Myra were already on the plane traveling from California, they charged me with finding a fourth person to fill the spot. It was already late afternoon. Who did I know that would say yes so quickly?

I had an idea. It was a long shot. At 6:00 PM, I sent Nick a text.

> Hi, Nick, this is crazy last minute, but I have been asked by friends to fill an empty seat at Rao's (one of Manhattan's toughest reservations to land) for a 9:15 PM reservation tonight. The couple who invited me are flying here from LA right now. They had invited another friend who dropped out sick a little while ago. They don't want her place to go empty. I don't want to ask anyone I am dating on such short notice. So, apologies for the spontaneity of this invite, but would you like to join us?

About an hour later, I heard from him. Stunning! Yes, he would like to go.

> That sounds good. I'm just leaving the office. Will be at the apt in thirty minutes or so. Let me know other details as necessary.

As he walked into the building at 7:45 PM, Nick called to find out the plans. I explained the jacket dress code and Rao's cash-only policy. Each of us would pay our own way. Signing off, we agreed to meet in 45 minutes by the elevator.

I threw on a simple black dress and grabbed a red and black cape in case the restaurant had the air conditioning cranked up.

Nick joined me at the elevator in a linen blazer, patterned blue button-down shirt, khaki slacks, and loafers. Perfect. At least we looked the part!

While riding the elevator down to the lobby, I called an Uber. Glancing at Nick, I was struck again with how much I enjoyed spending time with him. I was glad he was going to dinner. The evening would be comfortable and fun.

Texting Norm and Myra to let them know the seat was filled, I told them about Nick.

"We live practically next door to each other in my building. But we are just friends. So, please no inquisition. You'll enjoy him. It should be a pleasant evening. I'm just proud of myself for asking him!"

Nick and I beat them to the restaurant.

"Would you like a drink?" he asked, as we luckily found two empty bar stools next to each other in the packed restaurant. Our seats were great for people watching, even though the din of rock-and-roll oldies made it challenging to carry on a conversation. Already squeezed together, he had to lean in to hear what I was saying. Norm and Myra entered to find me smiling, with Nick's ear pressed against my face.

Our dinner talk flowed smoothly despite the commotion all around us. Seated in the middle of the room at a large round table that could have easily accommodated six, the four of us became the center of attention. Although we had no celebrity status, my California friends had worked their magic.

Even though Nick and I were seated on opposite sides of the table, the wait staff treated us as a couple. Making assumptions about our status, they asked Nick if he wanted to order for me. He smiled and took it in stride.

When Nick left the table for the men's room, Norm and Myra both spoke at the same time:

"He definitely seems interested in you in an understated way," Norm announced. "Agreed!" Myra chimed in. "Honestly, don't count him out!"

Now I was more confused than ever.

The Uber ride back to the apartment after dinner was easy. Nick and I repeated the drill of riding the elevator together to the 18th floor and saying goodnight in the hall. We hugged and adjourned to our separate apartments.

A week passed. I had a dinner invitation from another out-of-town couple. Originally, they were stopping by my apartment when they landed in Manhattan. But the traffic from the airport into the City was gridlocked. I suggested they skip the tour of my place, and I would meet them at the restaurant.

Now what to do with the hors d'oeuvres I had prepared for their visit? Standing in my kitchen, I momentarily thought about eating them. But then I had a better idea.

> Hi, Nick, are you home? This is going to sound crazy (like pretty much everything I do!). But here's the story: I'm going out for dinner at 7 PM with friends from Idaho. They planned to come by the apartment first, but now we are meeting at the restaurant. Bottom line: I made stuffed mushrooms that will not keep. If you are home, I would love to bring them to you.

Nick responded quickly.

> Yes, I'm here. Sure. Sounds good.

I knocked on his door 30 minutes later, dressed for my evening out. When Nick opened the door, I stood smiling, mushrooms in hand on a decorated platter.

"Wow," he said. "You go all out. Thank you. And you look great."

On the way back from dinner, my phone lit up with a message from him.

> Thanks for the mushrooms. They were a nice addition to my dinner. I'll return your container.

Summer was winding down, and the days were getting shorter. Nick sent me a message about getting together.

> Hi, Kate. How about Wednesday dinner? We can meet at the apartment and walk somewhere. Let me know if that works.

I picked a clubby steakhouse close by.

> Have you been to T-Bar on 3rd yet? Behold our Open Table reservation. We are in!

He responded with excitement:

> Nicely done. I approve!

I accepted the congratulations:

> You set a low bar for my success.

He answered, a bit confused:

> Thanks. (I think!)

The afternoon of our dinner, he texted me.

> I'm good for 7. Probably be a bit early. Meet you there. I am coming from work. See you soon.

A few minutes before walking out of the apartment, I sent him a message.

> I too am in work clothes. Dressed in black from head to toe like every other woman in NYC. Walking towards you now. I'll buy you a drink if I am more than seven minutes late. Our darn elevators are packed tonight—my excuse for not being prompt!

Nick answered immediately.

> No problem. I just arrived.

I found him standing at the U-shaped bar, holding a beer in a frosty mug, and talking with a young couple who were seated. Close by was a gregarious older woman of European descent who appeared to be floating from person to person. She immediately headed my way and latched on.

As Nick continued his conversation with the couple, she whispered conspiratorially to me: "I am Ursula from Bavaria. You don't look like you are from around here. But you got with the program quickly! Look, you are wearing all black. And, oh my! HE thinks you're fantastic," she said, gesturing not too subtly at Nick. "You two have something special, darling!"

I smiled. "Oh, there must be a mistake. We are truly just friends."

"No!" she said firmly. "I don't believe it. Just look at how he looks at you."

A few feet away, Nick caught my eye and then walked over to offer me a drink. I nursed the prosecco he brought me, as he finished his beer and got a second. With the restaurant's wait of thirty minutes for a seat, he and I each kept up our visits with the new friends in the bar.

Ursula demanded my full attention as she whispered loudly in my ear about Nick and me.

"He told me all about you before you walked in," she said. "Maybe he's just too shy to tell you how he feels."

When Nick and I were finally shown our seats, the table was so small neither of us could move without grazing our knees and legs against each other. I pretended not to notice.

"I have big news," Nick announced after we placed our orders. "I have started to date."

"How terrific for you!" I said, meaning it. "Tell me more."

For the next two-and-half hours, we shared stories about our dating adventures, analyzed the lessons we were learning, and talked about finding humor in each experience.

"It's not starting out that well for me!" Nick said. "My first date stood me up, and I had traveled all the way to Brooklyn to meet her. I waited two hours, finally gave up and ordered dinner I ate alone, and then came home."

"I'm sorry," I said. "It's a process. Be patient. It gets better."

After dinner, we took the long way back to the apartment building. Nick wanted to get cash from a bank ATM to pay me back for his dinner. And it was a nice night to be out. But it seemed at every turn, we kept bumping into each other without meaning to. Each time it happened, we would laugh it off, regain our footing, and keep walking.

As we said goodnight by the door to his apartment, Nick told me his brother and wife were visiting in a few days to see Broadway shows. "I would love your thoughts about what shows they should see. And I'd like for you to meet them if you are around when they get here."

"Give me a shout. My friend Kayla will be here from Texas to visit. Maybe we can all have a drink."

When Kayla arrived a few days later, I told her about the possible get-together with Nick and his family.

"Great! I'll figure out if he's interested in you, once and for all!" she exclaimed. "How could he not be?"

The very first afternoon of Kayla's visit, we ran into Nick by the elevator in our shared hallway. His brother and wife had already left, but he was game for a drink with us that evening.

Even before she and I made it back to my apartment, Kayla had rendered a decision.

"He's totally interested," she whispered, as if he could hear her with his apartment door closed. "When the three of us were talking just now, he was not even looking at me. Don't you see it?"

Later at the neighborhood wine bar, our new trio shared an animated conversation. I sat to Nick's left and Kayla was opposite us. We were seated in the middle of the happy hour crowd at a small table. During our second round of drinks, I felt Nick's hand accidentally brush my leg. I acted as if nothing had happened, but it unnerved me.

An hour later, Kayla and I made an exit to change clothes for our 8 PM dinner reservations. As we were saying goodbye, she suggested to Nick we meet again later if we got back early enough. "Yes, that would be fun," he agreed. "Anything before midnight. We barely got the conversation started."

Kayla and I returned from dinner feeling frisky. It was almost midnight. Poised with her hand ready to knock at his door, Kayla looked at me with a goofy grin. "No!" I mouthed quietly, pulling her towards my apartment.

The next morning over coffee, Kayla once again insisted Nick was attracted to me. I argued he wasn't. A few days later, she flew back to Texas, reiterating she knew best.

The day Kayla left, I was absentmindedly looking at my online dating feed, when Nick's profile popped up. Although we had shared dating stories, we had never seen each other's profiles.

I was fascinated to read his description of himself and scroll through the photos he chose. I could clearly see how women would find the profile appealing. Nick portrayed himself accurately. Authentic, easygoing, friendly, uncomplicated.

And in an instant, without meaning to, I swiped right.

Horrified, I realized I couldn't take it back. There was no doubt that he would see I had "liked" him. This felt too much like high school. I didn't want to paper over my mistake with a text.

The only way I could adequately address this goof was in person. Several days later, Nick and I went for a hamburger in the neighborhood. We settled on the neighborhood favorite J.G. Melon's and sat sipping drinks at the crowded bar.

"I don't know exactly how to bring this up," I half-yelled over the noise of the crowd. "I didn't mean to swipe right on your dating profile," I apologized, with a comical roll of the eye.

"Yes, I saw that," Nick said, in his relaxed way. "No harm done. There are no rules here. I am just glad we can keep sharing dating stories."

Over our burgers and waffle fries, he told me about a complicated work challenge he was facing. "I don't really have anyone else I can talk to about this," he explained. I listened carefully, offering encouragement and making a few suggestions. I also shared a new work initiative of my own.

We split the check and walked home.

When we returned to the building, Nick sent me a message:

> I had fun tonight. I enjoy talking with you. You're a very good listener and have sound advice drawn from your own experiences. Good luck with everything and talk to you soon.

I sent a fast reply:

> Thank you! And right back at you.

The next morning, I took a screenshot of the text Nick sent to me after our hamburger dinner. I wanted Kayla to render an opinion on the message.

> From Nick . . . do you think this exhibits ANY interest? He's very cordial, but I just don't know. . . .

Only that text didn't go to Kayla.

It went to Nick.

By mistake.

And now he would open my text (while he was at work!) and discover I was asking someone else if HE was interested in ME.

How embarrassing.

How irreversible.

How damning.

I had to find a way to recover and save the friendship. I thought for less than a second, and then typed a message:

> Nick, what you just received from me was intended for Kayla. There's nothing I can say here that will make this feel right, except please accept my apologies! I hope this exchange doesn't disrupt our friendship which is absolutely what's

> most important.

His reply was fast. Too fast.

> Okay, no problem. I will disregard. We can still be friends.

I felt worse.

So I sent another message.

> Thank you. That's what neighbors are for.
>
> The backstory here is that Kayla's opinion when she met you was that we might enjoy dating. I told her I didn't think it was smart, and that I doubted you were interested anyway. She asked again about us last night when she and I spoke on the phone. The text you just read was my response to her.

Nick responded.

> Okay. Being friends is what's right for me. If I were interested in a romantic relationship you would know. I do enjoy your company. I'm not in any way trying to be misleading about my intentions.

I answered, relieved.

> Yes, I thought I had interpreted it correctly. I agree friendship IS what's appropriate. I enjoy your company too, and you've never been misleading. And I really do hope you find your girl :).

His answer put us back on even footing.

> That's good. Thank you for the reassurance.

When his lease expired, Nick told me he was moving out of the building. "But I'll still be in the neighborhood and would love to stay in touch with you."

Before he moved we scheduled a goodbye lunch. As with all the times before, it was uncomplicated and friendly.

I had learned an important lesson.

Dating in your building IS complicated. Being friends is not.

And the couple who moved into apartment 18C just might be future recipients of a platter of stuffed mushrooms.

BRAEDEN the Banker

♪ If I Had a Hammer ♪

Artist: Pete Seeger

It was Dec. 26, one day after my car was totaled on Christmas Day.

The wreck had happened on my way to meet a date for a movie and Chinese food. Grateful to have plans my first Christmas in New York, I was also thrilled that the weather was beautiful for the late morning drive. The bright sun made the high wind and cold crispy air seem tolerable.

I had the radio cranked up loud, singing along to my favorite oldies. The iconic Temptations song "Get Ready" was playing. How appropriate for my date.

But the song foretold another event too.

Out of nowhere, on the almost empty highway, a small sedan raced up behind me and plowed into the back of my SUV. The impact propelled my car forward so powerfully that I slammed into the car in front of me.

The highway patrol officer assured me I wasn't at fault and asked if I thought my SUV was drivable. "I'll follow you if you think you can't get where you are going," he offered.

"Oh, no, I'll be fine," I responded, a bit shaken. Acting as if nothing had happened, I called my date to say I would be a "little late, but don't worry." Giving him a quick summary of the events, he quickly offered: 'I'll come get you."

"No, my Jezebella is tough. (I love naming cars for women.) "We will get there."

"Pray tell, why do you call her that?" he asked.

"Because she's so wicked cute!"

With the rear bumper barely attached, and my driver's side door not fully closing (I held it forcefully shut with my left hand the entire trip), Jezebella and I limped along another thirty minutes to Scarsdale.

During the movie, I couldn't help but think about the injuries to my vehicle. Two payments away from owning the car outright, I was attached to Jezebella as one of the last links to my former life in Texas. When she finally arrived on a flatbed truck in a snowstorm earlier in the year, I felt like New York was home.

Then, on a beautiful Christmas Day, this.

And now, a day later, my car was being towed.

Once my car was loaded onto the tow truck's flatbed, I climbed into the passenger side of the cab to accompany Jezebella to the body shop. Still thinking about the surreal events of Christmas and my precarious drive home with no functioning brake lights, I needed a distraction. The driver was peppering me with questions about the wreck, but I was barely answering. I had turned my attention to Bumble.

The driver kept up his patter. But I was looking down at my phone. At that moment, I was more interested in the profile of Braeden on a dating app than recounting what had happened to Jezebella in yesterday's holiday misfortune.

An image of a tall man pleasantly smiling, and dressed for the water on a boat's deck accompanied the profile. It read:

> Recently divorced man looking to start the rest of his life. Long Islander, work in midtown, well-traveled, educated, awesome father! Wall Streeter, fit, independent, beach lover, (not my boat!), funny. Love doing new things. I'm 6'5" so you can always wear your heels.

I loved the shamrock emoji that accompanied the message. This man didn't appear to take himself too seriously. And he must be Irish, with a name like Braeden.

I began composing a message, oblivious to the tow truck driver, who seemed to want to talk regardless of who was listening.

> Hi, Braeden, looks like you are having fun on that boat, no matter who it belongs to! You obviously have great friends. We could use some of those warm temps about now. This southern girl is freezing in New York!

He answered back immediately.

"Hi, Kate, this is Braeden Fitzpatrick."

"Hi, Braeden! An Irishman?!"

"Yes," he answered. "My parents were born there and came here separately. Met at a church dance in the Bronx. I grew up in Oyster Bay, one of ten children."

"Wow, I want to hear more," I said. "I was in a car wreck yesterday which involved a guy from Oyster Bay. Could this be bad luck? ;)"

"OMG. You ok?" Braeden sounded concerned. "I moved out of OB years ago. Not an omen . . . in fact, if you are free tonight, I'll buy you a drink to try to make up for my wicked brethren from my old hometown who spoiled your Christmas."

"That could be lovely," I answered. "My daughter comes in from Texas at 11 PM, so tonight is indeed my only window this week. Let's talk on the phone later today and figure it out."

Between calls with an insurance adjuster and a rental car agent, plus excitedly preparing for my daughter's late Christmas with me, I squeezed in an hour to talk to Braeden. A gentle, friendly voice on the phone, he was the same in person when we met later that evening.

His invitation was for a drink at 7 PM. The temperature had dropped to the lower teens. Even for the short drive to meet him, I dressed in multiple layers. Tights, jeans, turtleneck, vest, scarf, puffer coat, earmuffs, gloves, and snowboots—I was ready!

Arriving at the entrance of a sophisticated bar in a neighborhood hotel, I was thrilled to see a roaring fireplace inside. The leather banquettes and long tables were filled with people talking, eating, and having a good time. Elaborate Christmas decorations added an extra festive feel to the handsome lounge.

Waving from across the room, Braeden was half squeezed into one of the leather nail-studded swivel bar seats. With a protective arm over the empty one next to him, he had found a spot for both of us.

I maneuvered through the lounge crowd and made my way over to him. He stayed seated, afraid to lose his place. But I could tell even then, he was very tall. I patted his back and slid into the seat he had saved.

His smile was warm. "You made it!" he said, genuinely pleased. "Look what I got you." I turned to the bar where gleaming silver bowls of potato chips adorned the wooden ledge. He had claimed not one, but two, and placed them in front of us.

Paired with glasses of house Cab, the chips were too good to pass up, and we devoured the contents of both bowls. In seconds, they were refilled.

"I like this place!" I smiled. With all the excitement of the transport of my wrecked car to the body shop, securing a rental car, and getting everything ready for my daughter's visit, I hadn't eaten breakfast or lunch.

"How about a burger?" Braeden offered. I took another look at him. He must be 6' 5" at least. He was approachable and boyish in his sweater and jeans, and his eyes creased when he smiled. His voice was gentle, and his laugh was charming.

"Please! I'll be really tipsy if I don't eat, and I wouldn't want not to be responsible for what I say!" I answered, already feeling a bit loopy.

"That's a double negative," he chuckled, pointing out my grammatical error.

"I stand corrected! I DO want to take complete ownership of whatever I say. Bring on the burger," I urged.

Time flew. We talked and talked and talked.

After a second drink, our bellies full from mile-high burgers, and our conversation well lubricated, Braeden swiveled my chair around to face his. That's when I confirmed I was sitting next to a very big man. He looked at me and smiled. I smiled back. But I knew time was running out.

Glancing at my watch, it was close to 10 PM. I needed to leave to meet my daughter. I had learned a lot in the last three hours.

A dad to four young adults, Braeden was in banking, commuting by train every day to Manhattan from his home on Long Island. His daily exercise was the walk from Penn Station to his office on Park Avenue near the Met Life Building. Even though his bank was one of the largest financial institutions in the country and he held an important position there, Braeden struck me as completely down to earth.

More Long Island than Manhattan, Braeden explained he spent most of the time he wasn't working with his children, his extended family, or in an outdoor pursuit, like fishing or attending sporting events. One of the perks of his job was being in charge of distributing bank-purchased tickets to games for the Yankees, Mets, Knicks, and other sports teams in the area. He often hosted a bank box for VIP clients and could take his children and friends to the events.

Braeden was new to the dating world and hadn't had much experience meeting women. Newly divorced from his high school sweetheart, Braeden was just beginning to see women. Our date was the longest time he had spent with anyone since the summer.

"I really don't date much," he confessed. "I just got on a dating website because it is hard to meet people. I like Bumble because women make the first move. But now that I have gone out a few times, I realize that dating is expensive. I haven't relished the idea of one-night meetups, with dates who don't look at all like their pictures. And I don't enjoy spending money on women I will never see again."

"You seem so different from the other people I have met," he went on. "For one thing, you are grateful. You also come across as very genuine. After a few drinks, maybe you have me fooled. But my Irish intuition is pretty good! I would put my money on you, Kate!"

When we finally stood up to leave, I realized I was right about our mismatched size. Even if my snow boots somehow had heels, I was out of my league with Braeden. Seeing him stretch to his full height, I realized he was subconsciously bending his head ever so slightly forward to accommodate his size to mine.

"I guess everybody looks up to you!" I teased him, as we put our winter weather gear on.

"I am not intimidating," he said. "Far from it. I may be too nice."

"Well, you are that," I said, smiling. He took my hand in his and we headed outside. It was so cold we could see our frosty breath making circles in the frigid air.

I started to shiver.

We hurried to the parking lot to find my rental car. Braeden encircled me with his long arms as we stood under the hotel's garish white outdoor lights. I reached up as far as I could to put my arms around his neck and snuggled into his shoulder. When I looked up, our lips met. It was a very long, warm kiss. He bent down and engulfed me in a bear hug.

"So nice!" he sighed, as he let me go. "Have fun with your daughter. Talk soon."

On the drive to meet my daughter, I was as distracted as I had been with the chatty driver of the tow truck that morning. The big difference was then I had been looking at Braeden's picture on my phone. Now I had experienced Braeden's kiss in the parking lot.

Later that night, after my daughter and I had shared midnight cookies and hot chocolate, and she was tucked in bed, I checked my phone.

Braeden had sent me a message.

> Kate, I just got home.
> Hope your daughter is safe and sound. That was a great night and an even better kiss! We should've started saying goodbye much earlier! Perfect way to end the night.
> Looking forward to speaking soon.

I answered:

> Thanks so much, Braeden! I agree a kiss is one of the most important ingredients of chemistry. And I love knowing that you think ours was great! We didn't get close to finishing our conversation. But now that you know my last name, you could always Google me to see what's out there.

Braeden responded quickly:

> Kate, I'm not going to Google you, because what I see in front of me is more important/meaningful than the Internet. Good kiss. Yes! But not fully explored, because you were running the risk of being late and leaving your progeny in the cold. Need more data! Speak soon. Good night. Braeden

The days between Christmas and New Year's were busy with holiday activities planned for my daughter. Whether she and I were window shopping on 5th Avenue, attending the Rockettes Christmas Spectacular at Radio City Music Hall, or strolling through Central Park, Braeden was always checking in.

> Hope you two are having a great time. Don't forget that when your daughter leaves, I've offered to take you on a tour of my hood, the Long Island Gold Coast. We could start with Nassau County and the homes of the billionaires of yesterday and today!
>
> Also, by the way, I don't want to go on too much about the kiss . . . But it was the best thing that has happened to me in about three months. You solidified your reputation (new to me) as someone who is goal-oriented and takes initiative! Yes, well done.

Over the next few weeks, Braeden and I picked up the pace. We went out for Chinese food, to a movie, and coordinated our travel times in and out of Penn Station.

If our arrivals matched, we would look for each other in the enormous, swarming crowd near the ticket counters. I would enter from 34th Street and take an escalator down into the cavernous space. It was fun to play my own "Where's Waldo?" game to see if I could spot him. Because Braeden was so tall, he stood head and shoulders above 99% of the crowd. I usually found him near the giant board which flashed departure times and gates for the Long Island Railroad. He would be there, a foot taller than the others, scanning the crowd for me.

As soon as I got to him, Braeden would scoop me up in his arms, lifting me off the floor. When he kissed me, no one around us ever seemed to notice or care. We were anonymous in a sea of people, and our joyful PDA was none of their concern.

As Braeden had predicted, his schedule was busy. And, as he had shared, his family and work took priority.

Over many weeks, we would attempt to get together, but he had lots of plans.

> I think I can meet for a quick drink (and smooch?), but I'm going to Madison Square Garden with clients and our sales team for college basketball.
>
> I have lunch with my brother and his son about 2 o'clock so I don't think I can commit today.
>
> Hi. A burger and hug sound great. But I have plans with work colleagues. They are eager to have a drink with me after my Lenten alcohol cleanse and abstention!
>
> I could come by late on Saturday. Let me see what my kids want in terms of timing.

> I'm planning to go to Fairfield, Connecticut tomorrow for an early dinner to see my two sisters and a niece who lives nearby.
>
> I may "need" to go fishing Sunday morning, so it might be very late when I could see you.

And then later, after fishing, he wrote:

> The fish did not cooperate with my plan. But it was nice to feel the breeze again in my face. A little too late for me to come by now.
>
> My son and I had a sushi dinner in town, then we came back to my place and watched TV. Good times.
>
> I had a wake today for an old (age and longevity) family friend (93) who lived a good life. I was glad so many of us could be there.
>
> I'm at home now. Had dinner at my brother's. Another family picnic coming up on Sunday.
>
> I'm going for drinks with my work crew. Told my colleague Matt all about you. He approves.
>
> I just left Madison Square Garden watching the Knicks win. Heading down to Spring Street to see my Oyster Bay friend's daughter's art show. Tres chic.
>
> Hope you love this weather! In other news, my twins Seamus and Molly turn 21 today.

> I'm going to the Grateful Dead concert at Citi Field with my high school friends. Should be a good night.
>
> I have had a couple of hectic days getting ready for the Argentina trip with my kids. Can't believe we leave tomorrow. We are all very excited. Molly is grateful for the extra suitcase you gave me! Girls have lots of shoes and swimsuits. Ha!
>
> Just landed. Here's our crew . . . don't look much worse for the wear.
>
> Not easy to find the time or bandwidth in Argentina to text (literally, haha). Here's today's adventure! I am sure you are having your own in NYC. Can't wait to get caught up next month.

No doubt about it. Braeden's family obligations, ongoing work responsibilities, and travel had him always on the move. When we got together, it was usually in a narrow window he found in between. And sometimes the plans we made got canceled.

> Would you mind terribly if I took a rain check? I think I hit a wall. I was up at 5:15 this morning. And now I'm exhausted.
>
> I don't think it will be today. I'm just now getting on a train at Penn. And I have to shuttle my daughter from my place to hers. Long story, but she is still without a car.
>
> I deserve ten demerits, but I am going to have to cancel our Sunday plans. Just been given the opportunity to go to the Yankees game in the bank box. Have lots of tickets

> to give away. Taking my son, brother, nephew, and clients. Should be great fun, although we may freeze. Promise I'll make it up to you.

My response in every situation was always the same.

> Fantastic for you. Go enjoy!
>
> Love how much you love spending time with your family, and how fortunate for you that most of them are close by.
>
> Wow, that sounds amazing. Have fun!

Without fail, Braeden would send photos. He and his kids at his place celebrating a birthday. He and his daughter eating ice cream. He and another daughter in a canoe. He and his sons packing boxes to move a sibling, or assembling furniture for someone's new place. He and his brother with hammer and nails for a reconstruction project on a family condo in Florida. He and his pals at a Mets game. He and his family at a picnic. He and his children at the holidays.

> Kate, you are a wonderful sport about my schedule. And my children. I deserve a bucket of cold water thrown at me at times.
> How about this? You must have things you need done in your new place in Manhattan. Why don't you feed me dinner and I'll come over and put furniture together for you? It's a testosterone rush for me to do manly projects! ;)

It was an offer too good to pass up. Braeden's physical strength, experience with construction projects (his dad gave him and his nine siblings hammers even before they got to first grade), easygoing style, and desire for perfection were more than a match for all the chores in my new apartment.

I had been living there only for a couple of weeks, and the small space was already challenging my efficiency skills. No matter how much I played renter's organizational Tetris, my accumulation of personal effects, from books to dishes to shoes to makeup, took up more space than I had square footage.

I needed wall accessories for storage, cabinetry to hold bathroom products, furniture moved, and pictures hung. And the moving boxes I hadn't yet unpacked were heavy and unwieldy to break down. Plus, there were hardware repairs and touch-up painting that the apartment maintenance staff would only tackle if I seriously greased the wheel.

But Braeden would do it for grub!

We got into a rhythm. On Friday nights, I would throw together an easy meal. And wine. Always wine.

Braeden would pack shorts in his work backpack and pair them with the t-shirt under his dress shirt. "I sweat better with less on," he explained. "What's on the 'honey do' list tonight?"

For six weeks, he worked his way through every room in the apartment: fixing, improving, assembling, stacking, reorganizing, moving, and generously doing anything and everything I needed.

"I've burned lots of calories," he said. "I can eat totally guilt-free!" Braeden did the heavy lifting. I just stood by and offered moral support, ever the grateful cheerleader.

When he finished working, we ate pre-prepared or purchased comfort meals. He favored soups, mac and cheese, burgers, quiche, pasta, and pie. I would dig in too. Only I hadn't done anything to justify the calories!

After dinner, Braeden would head home on the late train to Long Island, energized and proud of his accomplishments. I, on the other hand, would feel like running around the block to burn off the huge food intake.

One Friday night, after he had spent hours laboriously putting together a mirrored jewelry chest, Braeden sent me a message on the train home:

> It's great to think your apartment is so suited to your lifestyle—welcoming, warm, functional, luxurious, sculptural, sensuous, mysterious. Oh, excuse me, my thoughts drifted off there at the end. Seriously, I truly enjoy your company and enjoy helping you make your beautiful apartment an even better oasis.

When we ran out of renovation and maintenance chores in the apartment, Braeden and I moved on to organizing my off-site storage unit. Manhattan Mini-Storage was in an area of the City I didn't know well and wouldn't frequent alone. What I needed—besides the heavy lifting to rearrange file cabinets, bins, and boxes—was a traveling companion for my storage jaunts.

Bella, my new SUV, lived in the parking garage which was attached to my building. The convenience of hauling things to and from my apartment, without going outside, was one of the top reasons I loved my building.

That Friday night, we packed the trunk of the car and drove the few miles to storage. The storage facility was multi-storied, with key card access to the building and each floor. Freight elevators were enormous, like hospital transport ones that could carry stretchers (or cadavers!). The whole place was creepy.

It always took two people to make a trip inside. One person watched the car at the loading dock and the other person secured a rolling cart from inside the building to use for the trip upstairs.

We filled the rolling cart with boxes and clothes from the apartment and took the elevator to the 8th floor. Once there, the concrete walls, harsh motion-activated lighting, and rows of narrow, claustrophobic aisles mimicked a prison. The hollow clang of the locks, which were mandated for each storage unit door, heightened the sense of foreboding and isolation.

But with Braeden, the experience was less intimidating and far more entertaining. Cracking jokes from the lobby to my unit, he was so comfortable and capable in that setting, I immediately relaxed. He knew how to maneuver the unwieldy cart and mastered opening the double locks on my storage unit door in seconds.

"Did you think about going into locksmithing?" I marveled. "You could gain entry, legally or illegally, to anything!"

"I AM pretty handy," he smiled, unloading the bags of clothes I was switching from my apartment to storage. After multiple trips back and forth to the car, we were thrilled to be finished.

"Can't wait for dinner," Braeden said. "I have been working up a sweat AND an appetite."

Headed back into the damp night air, I put my hand in the pocket of my fleece as we stepped off the elevator into the lobby. I couldn't feel my cell phone. It must be in the car, I thought, berating myself for leaving it in a place where it could be in danger of getting stolen.

Braeden put away the rolling cart, and I got in the car on the driver's side. Looking everywhere inside, I didn't see the phone.

When he opened the passenger side door of the car, Braeden quickly saw my look of despair. "You forgot something?" he said concerned, as he slipped into the passenger seat.

"No, worse," I said. "I can't find my cell phone. I could have sworn I brought it with us. I remember seeing it on the console of the car. Now, it's not here."

We went back upstairs to the storage unit and dug through everything. No cell phone there. We retraced our steps, coming in and out of the building. Not in the elevators or hallways either. We searched on the loading dock outside. No luck.

Now legitimately worried, I looked at him. "Do you think someone took it?"

"Not to panic," he said reassuringly. "We will go back to the apartment and look there."

Knowing he was starved, feeling guilty about how much extra time this was taking, and concerned about the phone's whereabouts, I looked up at him and mouthed "Thank you!"

In one swift motion, he grabbed me in his trademark giant bear hug and planted a kiss on the top of my forehead. "I promise we will find it," he pledged. And I believed him.

The trip back to the apartment was fruitless. We looked every place the phone could have been, but with no success.

Just as we were heading back out the door for one more return trip to storage, I had a brainstorm. I needed one more player in this mystery—my tech friend from Texas.

Borrowing Braeden's phone, I sent her a text.

"Hi, Julie, this is Kate. I know this isn't my cell number. I've lost my phone, and I need your help. Are you free?"

Within seconds, she called Braeden's phone back.

"What on earth are you doing, and whose phone is this?!" asked Julie. Always my right hand when I lived in the Lone Star State, Julie loved a challenge.

"Julie, meet Braeden. Braeden, meet Julie," I said, putting the call on speaker. "You two are my dream team tonight!"

"Ooh," she said when she heard the dilemma. "We are going to figure this out." Even though my phone was turned off, Julie had access through her computer to the Find My iPhone app.

Braeden and I got in the car. I drove while he opened up the app on his phone. Julie did the same on her computer and they compared notes.

She quickly picked up the signal for the location of my phone. Wow!

She and Braeden were now both tracking it. The signal showed it was a few blocks away.

"Drive!" he said. "We are going where the green dot blinks." He and Julie were quickly bonding over this new adventure.

But as I got to the location where we thought the phone was, the signal moved several blocks away. I would drive, and it would move again. I would drive to another new location, and it would move again.

After more than 30 minutes of this cat-and-mouse game all around my Manhattan neighborhood, Braeden had a thought.

"Pull over to the curb. I think the phone is in the car," he announced.

"But we searched the car," I countered.

"It takes a fresh pair of eyes, my dear. I am tackling this again."

Coming around to the driver's door, he turned on his phone's flashlight and began searching. My car was stopped in the middle of traffic in the right-hand lane of very busy Third Avenue. We were blocking everyone. Cars whizzed around us. Drivers honked and got far too close in their collective irritation.

I shuddered as I watched Braeden's 6' 5" frame contort, kneeling on the asphalt, digging with his hands under my driver's side car seat. Five minutes later, as more than a dozen cars had come precipitously close to careening into him and us, Braeden cried out triumphantly.

"I found it!" he yelled. "Quick, take it, and switch places with me. I am getting us out of here," he announced as he moved into the driver's seat and handed me the phone.

Half laughing, half crying, I ran around and jumped in the car on the passenger side as he negotiated his way back into the traffic.

"Incredible!" I gasped, back on the phone with Julie, who had been on speaker throughout the entire ordeal. "I don't know how to say thanks to you for standing by."

She started clapping. "Just picturing the two of you saved from nearly getting run over was enough entertainment for me," she said.

"Well, thank you again," I sighed in relief. "I'm taking Braeden to dinner. He deserves a couple of stiff drinks to start. This has been a long night already!"

"Just promise me more of your crazy stories the next time you're in Texas," Julie answered. "Glad you solved the mystery, Braeden!"

Over a steak dinner that evening, we laughed about the good fortune of him finding my phone.

"Yes! I was prepared to get my burglary tools, if necessary, to rip out your car seat. What does one wear to a party that's also a crime?" he joked.

"Is it my projects and predicaments that interest you most about me?" I asked him, smiling.

"It's all of it," Braeden answered. "You make even the challenges fun. I am slightly buzzed now. And I am also testosterone-depleted after all the excitement. But I want to go on record to say that I think after tonight I am even MORE glad you are in my life!! And now, since we've finished the apartment work, we can start watching Netflix on Friday nights!"

"What an interesting proposition!" I replied. "Will you know how to fix the cable if it goes out?"

"As long as I have tools, and you have the instruction manual, I am betting I can fix anything of yours," he answered confidently.

"Just give me a chance, Kate. I promise I'll bring my A-game. And, if needed, I am always happy to go to storage with you again. Maybe we'll get locked in!"

SAM the Solicitor

♫ Fly Me to The Moon ♫

Artist: Frank Sinatra

Not normally a morning person, I woke with a start at 5:30 AM. It was the last of four non-stop days. My boss Murray was in from Texas to make calls with me in New York City.

My role this week was taking the lead in arranging and preparing for our appointments. We were meeting with our most important national clients, so the stakes were high.

And for me, the challenges were even bigger than usual. Besides keeping up with the normally stratospheric pace of Murray's trips, I was also working remotely. Murray's travel coincided with my move to a new apartment. Only I wasn't moved in. I was in a hotel.

To mitigate the delay between when my things would arrive and the chaos I would need to unravel when they did, living in temporary space for a week seemed the best answer. But trying to stay organized and on track while feeling homeless was disorienting.

The day before I checked into the hotel, movers had dumped all my worldly possessions across town in the apartment. Preparing for Murray's arrival meant I hadn't had a spare moment to unpack anything. At least, I could create a semblance of normalcy at the hotel, without the distraction of seeing the tower of packing boxes at the apartment. There, my unmade bed was piled high with clothes, and my refrigerator was empty.

So now, this unfamiliar hotel in an unknown city was home away from home while I worked around the clock with Murray.

The May morning was hot and sticky. I could feel the humidity even through the windows. What could I wear to look professional on this uncomfortably oppressive New York day?

Planning ahead, I packed a suitcase for my temporary residence at the hotel. Dress for the meetings I lined up was summer business casual. I hoped I had enough clothes to mix and match.

But I hadn't counted on two things:

1) I got rained on twice, rendering two of my three jackets completely out of shape, and all but one pair of pants impossibly wrinkled.

2) On his own, Murray had added a meeting with our biggest client and invited me to attend. It was today. The attire was strictly business.

Peering in the hotel closet, I took out the only clothes I had left. A three-quarter-length dark denim jacket paired with a cream ribbed tank top was marginally acceptable. A strand of chunky artisan pearls only improved it slightly. My too slim black straight-legged slacks were better suited to drinks and dinner in a dark restaurant than a meeting in daylight. I hoped that somehow my conservative black pumps would pull it all together.

I had only heard tales about the man Murray scheduled us to see. Sam Church was a legend. The gatekeeper and chief of staff for a billionaire entrepreneur, Sam himself was a Harvard grad, a brilliant and serious executive, admired, and maybe even feared. Nine years before, the billionaire had handpicked Sam to set up and manage his business operations, both professional and personal.

Murray and I were going to make a pitch. The trouble was, I didn't know how I would contribute to the conversation. Murray had the distinct advantage of a prior relationship with Sam. For all I knew, Sam didn't even know Murray was bringing me with him.

"I'll do the talking," Murray said, as he gave me a quick briefing when we disembarked from the taxi in front of Sam's building. The address on Madison Avenue is home to the offices of many of the wealthiest individuals in New York City.

The twenty-five storied limestone and granite building is both understated and elegant. At the entrance, a ten-foot-tall bronze of Frederic Auguste Bartholdi's Statue of Liberty sets the tone for the stature of tenants who work inside.

I could hear my footsteps tap the marble floor as Murray and I approached the security desk.

"Act like you know what you are doing," I told myself, as I glanced at the soaring ceilings, trying not to gawk. Smiling pleasantly, I showed my ID to the security guard. He glanced at it, then glimpsed at me, and smiled back.

Whew! I passed muster. But this is only step one.

After Murray handed over his ID, the guard placed a call to Sam's office, announcing our arrival to the building. "Mr. Church will see you now. Please take the elevator to the 18th floor." He directed Murray and me to a corridor across the lobby.

On the way to the elevator bank, Murray and I passed a roped-off display of three 16th Century Knights of Armor. Amazing! In the lobby of a New York City office building, I was encountering a lifelike representation of medieval King Arthur's Court, like in *Camelot*.

I snapped a photo.

Why not? This was my new life, and I was relishing it.

Murray had walked on towards the elevators. As I rushed to catch up, I glanced at the wall ahead. An original full-length portrait of George Washington, by artist Gilbert Stuart, hung behind a glass case. The lobby was a virtual museum!

I mentally pinched myself as we rode the lightning-speed elevator to the 18th floor. The doors opened to a sleek glass and mirrored hallway, far more contemporary than the elegant and old-world feel of the downstairs reception area.

Just to our left, an attractive and well-dressed young woman motioned us through double glass doors opposite the elevators. "Mr. Church is expecting you," she said.

With an inviting coffee bar, a white marble island was the centerpiece of the large gray and white office suite. A barista stood behind the serving station, offering coffee, tea, juice, fruit, and croissants. With my adrenaline fueling enough nervous energy, I declined the offer of food and drink. Murray accepted a shiny white mug filled with hot coffee as we followed the receptionist down a hallway.

The sophisticated suite of offices was light, open, and airy, with glass walls providing a peek into spacious individual workstations on either side of the hall. Large museum-quality photographs of black-and-white landscapes were on display throughout, suggesting that a serious collector had been at work.

Our guide showed us to a small but elegant room. It held two pairs of upholstered chairs, positioned opposite each other. There was no desk or conference table. An expensive patterned foot rug provided the visual break between the two seating areas.

Murray and I took the pair of chairs facing inward towards the door. That would leave Sam to choose a seat in the opposite pair, directly across from one of us, and looking out of the expansive windows towards Central Park.

Leaning against the wall next to Murray was another massive framed black-and-white photo. The camera had captured a snow-capped mountain range in great detail. "It's Ansel Adams," I said to Murray. "This is quite the collection."

"Only a fraction of what we have here in the office," said a male voice from across the room. I turned away from the photograph to look.

Walking into the room was a tall, slender, handsome man who easily could have been on the cover of a fashion magazine. I took it all in. His black, double-breasted, European-cut suit, starched white shirt with mother-of-pearl cuff links, and his polished black wingtips were an impressive sight.

He filled the space with a commanding physical presence. No one would have ignored Sam Church, least of all me.

He extended his hand first to me and smiled slightly. "Hello, I am Sam Church," he said with authority. "You are?"

"Kate Somerset," I replied, still holding onto his hand and looking him straight in the eye. "Very good," he said, and then turned to Murray.

"Welcome back, Murray. Let's have a seat and you can tell me what you came to discuss," Sam said matter-of-factly. He took the chair opposite Murray and crossed his long legs towards me.

Murray began speaking.

Trying not to stare at Sam as I listened to Murray talk, I occasionally caught Sam stealing glances at me. I attempted to ignore it, but there was a moment when our eyes met.

Sam abruptly broke away from the conversation with Murray, turned to me, and said: "Kate, what is your role in this effort?"

Smiling, I replied: "Going forward, I will be the firm's new contact in New York City. It's a pleasure to meet you and to hear more about what you do here. I have a lot to learn since I've recently moved alone from Texas to Manhattan."

"Ah," he said. "Welcome! That's a bold step to come from Texas. I think you'll enjoy Manhattan, and if there's anything I can help with, let me know. I've been divorced for a number of years and find it's an interesting place to be single."

The dynamics had just shifted.

Here is a single man, looking like a movie star, engaging me in thoughtful conversation. "Enjoy this in the moment," I reminded myself.

For the remainder of the meeting, I chimed into the discussion in ways I hadn't expected I could. And Sam listened and nodded, giving equal attention to both Murray and me. But his gaze was often on me, and he knew that I knew it.

An hour-and-a-half passed, far more than the time we had been allotted. Sam stood up to close the meeting. Murray and I rose on cue.

My legs felt weak, and my skin was tingly.

Please don't let this be a moment to shake hands again. No way will I appear cool and collected with clammy hands!

"I have another meeting in a few moments, but I'd be more than happy to give you a fast tour of our offices," Sam said. "We just moved in, and I'm afraid we're not as organized as I'd like. We have one room that is warehousing our collection of Ansel Adams photographs. Would you like to see it?"

"What a treat!" I jumped in. "I'm amazed at the incredible images we've seen so far. How lucky you are to be surrounded by such beautiful art."

"I never take it for granted," Sam said. "I always have to remind myself it's not my collection, it's not my money, but it IS my responsibility!"

The tour took another twenty minutes. Walking us back to the entry, Sam asked Murray if he would like a refill on coffee. And to me, he offered 'whatever strikes your fancy' accompanied by a sweeping hand gesture of the tempting array of drinks and snacks. Smiling, Murray and I both declined with thanks.

As we were leaving, Sam shook Murray's hand. He then took my extended hand in both of his and squeezed it. His dark eyes gazed intently into mine. His hands lingered over my hand a microsecond longer than would've been expected for a business handshake.

"Again, what a pleasure," he said, directed to me. "I'm glad you're in New York, and thanks for coming to see me."

Murray and I retraced our steps in reverse to leave the building, this time not stopping to admire the art in the lobby. Only when we were outside waiting for a taxi did Murray speak:

"Well, Kate, that was a good meeting on two fronts. First, Sam really listened to us. In particular, you made valuable contributions. I'm glad I asked you to come with me.

Secondly, I'm quite sure he was glad I asked you to join us. In fact, it seems entirely possible you'll be getting some additional insights into what makes him tick. I think there's a date waiting to happen," he smiled at me.

"Really?" I said, surprised. "It's obvious that Sam is a powerful presence in this city for his business acumen. And I can't even imagine what kind of demand he is in as a single man. Given the circles he runs in, I doubt he would even consider pursuing a newcomer in town."

Murray disagreed. "I'm going to fall on my sword on this one. You'll hear from him."

Two hours later, an email arrived from Sam.

"Dear Kate and Murray," it began, with my name first.

"It was a pleasure to see you today . . ."

Murray and I responded separately. While I wanted to keep my message professional, I also wanted to reference Sam's offer of help to me as a newcomer to NYC.

"Sam, thank you for giving us so much time today to discuss our work initiative," I wrote in part. "I am going to take you up on your offer to be a resource, as I make my transition from Texan to New Yorker. You've already been more than gracious, but I never say no to great advice."

Sam acknowledged both Murray's and my email responses, continuing to put my name first when he wrote to us jointly.

A few weeks passed. Then a more personal email arrived from Sam.

"How's New York treating you?"

"Great!" I responded, "And it would be even better if I knew everything you know about the people who make this City run. Any chance you'd be willing to share chapter one?"

"Indeed, I am an open book. Ping me when you are available."

Thrilled, I answered with several options of dates when I was free. A week later, Sam suggested we meet for dinner.

He invited me to Perrine, the signature restaurant at the Pierre Hotel on Fifth Avenue.

I arrived first, stepping into the entrance out of a drizzle, brushing water droplets from my shirred watercolor patterned dress. With no umbrella or raincoat, I was again an unprepared victim of a summer shower. When Sam walked in behind me, I was still smoothing my hair.

"Hello, Kate," he said, smiling. I drew in a breath and smiled back.

Lightly touching my shoulder, he followed behind me as the maître d' led us to the secluded back corner of the restaurant.

"Here we are, Mr. Church. I trust your table works for you this evening."

"Of course, Richie," he said. "Please bring the lady a hand towel, so we may get her dry from the city showers." In seconds, Richie returned with an embossed guest towel bearing the restaurant's medallion. I dabbed at the water on my clothing, while he stood waiting patiently.

"Thank you, Richie," I said.

Satisfied I was taken care of, Sam pulled the leather chair out for me. I looked around. Old school and old New York, the famed French-American restaurant was richly appointed and elegantly plush, with wait staff donned in tuxedos gliding from table to table. Around the perimeter brass rail hung half curtains made of lace, providing privacy for each dining section.

Menus were placed in front of us, but mine had no prices on it.

"May I order for you? I am somewhat of a regular," he winked.

The comfortable banter between Sam and Richie continued as Sam made our dinner selections. Antonio, our waiter, knew him too. I was impressed that he was not just courteous to both, but also interested in them too.

Our meal was delicious, and time flew by. Sam talked about work responsibilities, life in New York, his two daughters, and asked probing questions about me, my daughter, and my impressions of Manhattan.

After we passed on dessert, as tempting as it was, I knew our evening was drawing to a close.

"Thank you so much for a lovely experience," I said, as Sam paid the bill. "You were so gracious with your time. I appreciate your attempt to bring a New York stranger up to speed."

"This is just the beginning, Kate," he said. "I hope we can do it again. Now let's get you an Uber. I'll ride with you to your building and then on to my apartment. Just enter your address into my app."

It was a surprising and gallant gesture. And, of course, it also let him know where I lived.

Waiting for the car, we stepped outside to discover it was still raining. I had paid no attention to the weather during dinner. Out of nowhere, Sam opened an umbrella above my head and said:

"I can't have a lovely Texan get wet on my watch."

When the car pulled up to the curb, Sam opened the rear passenger door for me, holding the umbrella over my head to ensure I would stay dry. Then in one fluid motion, he walked around to the driver's side of the car, got in the back seat, and closed the umbrella, while keeping all the rain droplets away from me.

Introducing himself to the Uber driver, Sam kept up a friendly conversation with him on the short trip to my building.

As the Uber pulled up in front, Sam squeezed my hand, saying: "Don't move!" He got out of the car, walked around to open my door, and then extended a hand to pull me out.

Stepping onto the sidewalk in front of my building, I faced him. He reached forward and hugged me, and then followed with a soft kiss on the cheek.

"Ciao, Kate. Until next time," he whispered in my ear. I turned back to say goodbye, and he disappeared into the car with a wave.

The next Thursday, Sam left me a voicemail.

"Hi, Kate. This is Sam Church. I have tickets to see a set at the Jazz Standard tomorrow night. I know it's last minute, but hope you can go with me."

He was asking me out on Thursday for a Friday night. That wasn't much notice. Did someone cancel on him?

"Oh, Sam, I'm disappointed I can't," I answered, semi-relieved I had a conflict. "I really want to do this! But my daughter comes tomorrow from Texas for the weekend. Darn! Can you give me a little more notice next time? I promise to block off my calendar. I would love to see you!"

Back came his reply. "Sorry. My daughter bagged me at the last minute. I promise to call ahead next time. Have fun with your daughter. Cheers!"

"It's really OK. I would always rather be asked," I assured him. "Hope you have a great weekend."

Over the next two weeks, Sam made several more last-minute attempts for another date, but I always had other plans.

I kept my answers grateful and interested.

"It looks like such fun."

"Thank you again for thinking of me."

"So sorry I'm not available."

"Not to be totally presumptuous, but do you ever go out on 'school nights'?" I asked. "My next three weekends are ridiculous. In contrast, it's calm during the week. Just wanted to let you know. I figure if you ask me out again, and I can't go, you'll forget my name!"

"Not a chance!" Sam answered. "How about dinner Monday night? We might want to change into casual clothes and meet in the neighborhood. How's the French restaurant Orsay?"

Perfect. We could finally make it work.

Over a meal of artichokes and fish, Sam leaned across the table to hold my hand. The gesture made me swoon.

But I had to know. Why was a man seemingly with so much to offer available? By all logical accounts, he shouldn't be single.

"So, tell me, how is it that someone like you is not in a relationship?" I asked.

Looking me straight in the eye, Sam responded forthrightly. "I do have a woman I have dated, but she's in Chicago. We see each other off and on."

We finished our meal, and Sam suggested we walk together back to my apartment. Hand in hand, we traversed Manhattan's side streets, lit by streetlamps, populated by quaint storefronts and brownstones, and filled with groups of people on the sidewalks chattering amiably.

Ever the gentleman, he steered me over uneven concrete, through busy intersections, and around pedestrians that weren't moving at our fast clip. When we arrived at my building fifteen minutes later, he asked if he could come in.

Wavering for a moment, but feeling the undeniable chemistry I had experienced since the moment we met, I said yes. Riding up in the elevator to my apartment, I couldn't decide what I wanted to happen or know for sure what Sam had in mind.

He made it easy for me. "I want to see the view from the balcony you mentioned you never use. I know you are on the 18th floor," he smiled. "Just like in my office building, but of course, with an entirely different view. Just too bad for me, I don't get to look at you every day," he added.

Walking to the end of my living room, he slid the heavy glass doors open. "Lucky you!" he said, as he stepped out onto my small balcony and walked over to the iron railing. From that vantage point, he was looking towards the lights of the 59th Street Bridge. He took my hand and pulled me over the lip of the door to join him.

"Honestly, I'm scared of heights, so I'm not out here very much," I confessed. He gathered me close to him and whispered:

"Close your eyes and look up at me. I'll keep you safe."

I moved in closer. I felt his lips on mine. The kiss started tenderly and then picked up heat. For a moment, I forgot where I was. From below, I could hear the sounds of the city. The soft summer breezes had grown cool and the stars sparkled faintly in the sky.

"Wow!" he said, slightly separating away from me. "I think I could get into trouble here."

"Oh, I am not a troublemaker. I grew up Catholic," I winked. "You know, lead us not into temptation . . ."

A few kisses later, and he was heading towards my door, thanking me for the evening.

Through the summer months, there were more get-togethers and more kissing. At the end of each date, I'd hear: "Kate, you are beautiful. Ciao until next time."

Stepping up the public face of our dates, Sam asked me to accompany him to a formal event at the University Club on Fifth Avenue. Built in the late 1800s, the architecture of the multi-storied building is Italian-style Renaissance. With dark woods, painted mural ceilings, a renowned library, and an extensive art collection, the Club is quintessential New York City.

The evening's soiree was a swing dance for club members and their guests. Held in the formal dining room with forty-foot ceilings, enormous brass chandeliers, and a wooden dance floor with full orchestra boxes, the party was being staged in the most perfect place for an elegant evening.

Satin burgundy bedecked serpentine food stations, multiple bars, and candlelit tables for ten were set for a well-groomed crowd. I was glad I owned a glittery silver organza dance skirt. Paired with a black crinkle camisole and shrug, and a slim rhinestone buckle belt, the look worked on the dance floor.

And that's where Sam wanted to be.

Taking me by the hand between each of the dinner's five courses, Sam led me to dance with his arm securely circling my waist. Whirling around to the tunes of Frank Sinatra and Tony Bennett, we barely sat long enough to meet our tablemates, let alone eat dinner.

The entire evening was a dream sequence. I wondered if I had been transported to a movie set. As if written into the script, Sam was the romantic lead with both courtly, good manners, and suave seduction skills.

Excusing myself to the powder room to reapply my lipstick after dessert, Sam left the table too. When I stepped back into the hallway to return to the dining room, he was suddenly there. Pressing me up against the wall, he kissed me passionately. "You are delicious," he murmured. "I can't wait to get out of here."

In the Uber on the way home, we were all hands. I felt a rush in my stomach and a sense of heightened anticipation.

Returning to my apartment, we plopped on the couch in the living room and he began feverishly kissing me.

After a few minutes, I reluctantly pulled away. I breathed deeply to disengage from the steamy scene that was unfolding.

"Before we go further," I said softly, "would your friend in Chicago be happy about this? If you are not engaged or planning to marry, and I'm not interrupting a committed relationship, then great. But if even part of you thinks she would not want me in this equation, I think we ought to hit pause."

Sam pulled away. "You know, you are right," he admitted. "This is difficult. I love your company. And you know how attracted I am to you. I guess I should say thank you for helping me think about this correctly, even though I don't want to," he sighed.

That was our last official date. Sam took me to brunch at the

Four Seasons several weeks later. Our talk lasted three hours. The chemistry was still there. But it was time to put on the brakes.

Over eggs benedict and champagne, we reluctantly transitioned from romantic attachment to friendship.

When I got back to my apartment, I sent him a message:

"Thank you very much for today. Every time I'm with you I find myself getting goosebumps. (OK, not the whole time, but often!) Seriously, breakfast/brunch/lunch was incredible. And the conversation was even better. I love your energy, your vitality, and your take on living a big life. Safe going on all your adventures. I'm counting you in all the really good things that happened for me this year."

Answered Sam:

"I'll never forget you, Kate. The day you walked into my office, you completely distracted me. And I still am. So, Ciao for now. Thank you for your kindness and your trust in me. You are no stranger to New York anymore. You took me and the City by storm."

CHRISTOPHER the Connoisseur

♫ I Think We're Alone Now ♫

Artist: Tommy James and the Shondells

The May day was hot and sticky, even though summer hadn't officially arrived. I had dressed for a cocktail party before I left home. Although it was just mid-morning, I was already dabbing at my forehead, and methodically moving my hair away from the back of my neck as I waited for the train.

Once on board, I deeply regretted the decision to wear pantyhose, which were now stuck to my dress, which was now stuck to the train car seat. The term "climate-controlled" to describe the train cars was hyperbole. They were always stuffy, and either too cold or too hot.

In today's case, the humid air outside seemed to have worked its way inside, made only more miserable by an A/C system permanently stuck on tepid.

There were hours more to go before my evening event.

It was going to be a long day.

To other riders on my train, it was obvious I wasn't dressed like a work commuter. My black wraparound silk dress was both inappropriate for a train ride and awkwardly stuck to my legs above my knees, making sitting almost immodest.

The three-quarter-length sleeves each had four fashion-forward, silver-ringed grommets, a perfect look for cocktail party attire, but not exactly de rigueur for a train ride into Manhattan.

At each stop, embarking and disembarking commuters looked at me and my dress with a hint of disinterested puzzlement or even thinly concealed disdain. I smiled back as if I had no idea why they were staring.

My train seat was directly opposite a businessman who glanced fleetingly at me from above his tablet as I took my place.

I had stepped into the packed car, without a game plan for where to sit. Feeling lucky to find anything open, I had slid sideways into an aisle seat and only then realized that my row of chairs faced the handsome stranger.

When I turned my body forward, there he was, his long-legged body angled towards me. I crossed my legs to avoid stepping on his expensive tasseled dress shoes and shifted my body back towards the aisle.

That's when I caught a sideways glimpse of him looking my way again. Although it was brief, he seemed to take me all in, and then he quickly looked down at his tablet again. It was as if he couldn't decide whether he wanted to hold my gaze or turn away.

I pretended not to notice. I counted the times I caught him casting his eyes towards me. It seemed he was both looking at me, and also to the side of me, closest to the aisle.

Once.

Again.

A third time.

On that third time, I realized he wasn't looking at me at all. His eyes were fixed on a spot on the floor just beneath me.

As he gazed down, it was the perfect opportunity for me to quickly glance at him. His eyes were the color of ocean water. His lashes were long. His hair was richly textured, a silver salt and pepper shade, with so much body it could star in a shampoo commercial. He wore a French blue button-down shirt, and his dark gray slacks were impeccably pressed. A navy blazer was slung over his long legs.

In what seemed like the briefest time, the train conductor's voice on the PA system announced our pending arrival into Penn Station. At the same moment, my riding companion swiftly reached down and towards my legs.

I instinctively jumped back more deeply into my seat. His movement was so lightning fast I didn't have time to consider what was happening, as he scooped something off the floor from right under my feet.

Leaning towards me with a faint smile, he opened his hand.

"Is this yours?" he asked with a twinkle in his eyes, staring right at me. His gaze took my breath away.

It took me a second to redirect my eyes towards his open palm. In it was a shiny silver orb.

Now it was my turn to stare.

What could this be? I wondered. It was metal in the shape of a circle.

"I don't know," I answered. "I mean, I don't think so."

He touched me lightly on my right forearm. "Look above my hand," he said, now smiling broadly.

"I believe you've lost something."

The handsome stranger was indeed right! Where the top sleeve grommet had been near my right shoulder, now just my skin was showing, surrounded by a black fabric hole. He was holding the grommet in his hand.

"Quite the fashion statement you are making there," he laughed. "Got a tailor in the City?"

"I don't have anything in the City yet," I answered. "I'm just moving into a new apartment and picking up my keys today. Wow, will THEY be impressed I'm arriving with part of my dress missing.

"I can assure you they will," he said with a serious expression. "Anything I can do to help you?"

"Yes!" I laughed. "Tell me how noticeable this is."

"Well, I noticed it," he said. "Does that answer your question? Besides, it's my business to notice these things. I was in the fashion industry for most of my career. Technically, I was in men's footwear, but I pay attention to all details with any attire.

And once I've seen it, I can't unsee it. I'll remember your dress sleeve. And I would put money on the fact I'll also remember you," he finished coyly.

More amused than flustered at my dress predicament and what that would mean for my day, I pulled out my business card. "I'm Kate," I said. "If you can think of a solution for my wardrobe challenge, I will be all ears."

"You're not all ears," he replied. "In fact, I haven't even noticed your ears. But I can tell you what kind of shoes you are wearing."

"You mean the make?" I asked, now feeling embarrassed I didn't have on particularly great footwear. Before I could explain that I'd have a very long day with lots of walking in advance of the evening cocktail event, my riding companion answered.

"Those are two-panel shoes. And I am Christopher. Now you have double the information you started with on your train ride today."

"What's a two-panel shoe?" I asked, incredulous.

"It's a shoe that's made with more than one piece of leather," he answered.

"Is that good or bad?" I wanted to know.

"Depends," he said. "But I'll need to explain another time. We're going to have to get off the train."

Quickly, I gathered my belongings, still holding the grommet in my hand. The full weight of my sartorial problem was beginning to hit me. Christopher had all but admitted my dress had lost some of its charm. And I had no alternative but to wear it all day and into the evening.

As we stepped off the train together to exit into the crowded corridors of Penn Station, Christopher extended his hand. "Kate, it's nice to meet you. Welcome to New York City. I hope you enjoy your life here. And look at it this way, you are making quite the entrance! You'd stand out wherever you are, and today now more than ever."

Switching the grommet from my right hand to my left, I clutched it as I shook Christopher's hand and took the business card he offered.

"I have a feeling this is just the beginning of an adventure," I said sincerely. "I also have the feeling I might need more of your advice. Please don't lose my card!"

"Deal!" Christopher promised as I hurried away, marveling over what would have happened if he hadn't found the grommet, and we had not had a reason to meet.

Still thinking about the coincidence, I raced through the train station's warren-like corridors with low ceilings, harsh fluorescent lighting, streams of people walking in no particular pattern, and then ran up two staircases and an escalator, all to surface back outside into the heat.

In the taxi queue line, I reflected.

Was Christopher single?

Had he even noticed ME, or was he only trying to get the missing piece of my dress back to its rightful owner?

Would he hang onto my business card, or would it go into a giant collection of other impromptu contacts he had made and forgotten?

Would I ever see him again?

My next stop was the apartment building to pick up my keys and meet the staff. The taxi delivered me to the front door where a uniformed doorman who introduced himself as Jesse greeted me.

"Hi, I'm Kate," I said. "I'm new to the building and already need some help. I've lost part of my dress!" I announced, holding out the grommet. "See, it goes here," I pointed to the hole in my right sleeve. "Do you think there is anyone who can help me push it through to the other side?"

"Well, young lady," Jesse said, raising his eyebrows amusedly. "I have been here thirty years. And this is the first time I have been asked this particular question. Let me send you to Maria, our building manager. She will give you your keys, and perhaps she can help you out with this unique issue."

With a hopeful spirit, l headed downstairs to Maria's office. As I approached the door, I could see her through the glass window. With a cellphone to one ear, desk phone to the other, scribbling furiously on a document, and piles of paper everywhere, Maria looked like a modern-day version of a harried telegraph operator single-handedly managing an old-fashioned company switchboard.

Red reading glasses perched precariously on her nose, her thick coarse shoulder-length blond hair tousled, one hoop earring removed and tossed aside, and each wrist full of bangle bracelets, Maria was both askew and unaware that I was observing her.

Since I had been told by the doorman to walk right in, I grabbed the doorknob, pushed opened the heavy metal door, and walked the foot and a half to stand in front of Maria's desk. Still, on the phone, her quick distracted look up at me suggested I would not be an immediate priority.

I couldn't help but overhear her side of the call. "Yes, yes, a thousand times, yes. I need a plumber to look at every apartment in the E line. We must find that gas leak today. I don't care that he's not in the area now. Get him back ASAP!!" Maria growled.

Even as she hung up the office phone, and simultaneously tossed her cellphone on a tall stack of teetering file folders, Maria didn't look relieved. Finally, she raised her eyes to me, her face in a permanent frown.

"Yes, what are you here for?" she barked.

"I am the new tenant in 18A," I said, pleasantly. "I came for my keys. But I also must ask a big favor. Do you think you could help me with my dress?"

And pointing at my right shoulder and the ever-enlarging hole where the grommet used to be, I sucked in my breath in dismay. Now the grommet directly below the missing one was loose, hanging only by a thread. That meant only two grommets out of four remained intact.

"Do you have any scotch tape?" I asked, not waiting for an answer. "You see, I was thinking that if you could put your hand under my dress and lift the fabric from the inside, I could slide this metal piece back in place. Then we could try to tape it."

It was either my naïveté in asking her to assist, or the sheer implausibility of my solution, but Maria's facemask of irritability suddenly cracked. "I don't even know you," she said amusedly. "But any other woman who lived in this building and came in here in your condition would be in tears. How are you so calm? I tell you it's refreshing!"

Together we tried the emergency fix on my sleeve. Not only did it not work, but the tugging and pulling caused the second grommet to slip out of place for good.

"You either need to change clothes or go get a sweater," Maria declared.

"Not happening," I said. "I don't live in this building yet, so I have no change of clothes, and it's 85 degrees outside, and climbing . . . with 150% humidity! So, I don't plan to go buy a sweater either."

"Okay, go right next door at this level to the dry cleaners and see if they can help you," Maria offered. "They might have a special tool. Or maybe they can send you to a tailor."

Tailor! The word made me think of Christopher. Did he even remember this morning?

After I picked up my apartment keys and said goodbye to Maria, I made a failed attempt at the cleaners next door. Still thinking of Christopher, I tripped inside the tiny entryway, falling back against the lone light switch, which plunged the entire shop into darkness. I kept laughing until I could recover my balance, find the wall switch, and flip it back on.

Offering an apology, I introduced myself. "Hi, I'm Kate in 18A. Maria sent me. Take a look," I said, gesturing towards my now badly damaged sleeve.

"You're not from around here, are you?!" Constantino, the owner, said.

"How did you know?" I played dumb.

"Let's start with your accent, then we can move onto your style of dress, and we will end with your grand entrance just now!" Constantino responded. "I have to hand it to you, though. You've never stopped smiling the whole time."

Assessing my arm, he went on. "I am sorry, but this is going to be strike two. I can't fix that sleeve. My suggestion is to let me remove the other two grommets, and you'll have one arm with, and one without. Tell everybody the dress was made that way."

Reluctantly, I let Constantino perform the grommet surgery

on the right sleeve and tucked the four metal circles in my purse. Time was flying as I went upstairs to my empty apartment to look around.

On impulse, I opened a kitchen cabinet and placed all four grommets on the first shelf. Then I sat on a windowsill and sent Christopher a text.

"Since I met you this morning, you've put in motion a lively chain of events. Why didn't you tell me my new life in New York was going to be so adventure-filled?"

Two minutes later, he answered.

"Ah, the girl on the train with the holy arm. I was hoping you made it to your destination. Do tell. What is this lively chain of events?"

"Meet me for a drink, and I'll tell you," I said on a whim. "That is, if you're single," I added, holding my breath.

Again, minutes later, Christopher answered. "I'm headed to an event downtown. But it just so happens I have an hour free before. And after our encounter today, I'm just curious enough about what happened to you to consider being late.

Meet me at The Monkey Bar in an hour. And yes, I am single."

An hour later, a taxi deposited me at the door of the iconic midtown New York establishment. With the sophisticated atmosphere of a 1920s retrofitted jazz club, the Monkey Bar's painted mural walls, red velvet curtains, and deep wood-grained paneling is the perfect setting for a rom-com rendezvous.

Peering through the stylish happy hour crowd, I could see Christopher sitting with his back to me on a red leather stool at the elegant brass bar rail. I'd know that silver-peppered hair anywhere!

He pivoted in place in the direction of the room at the exact moment I saw him. I was standing transfixed, absorbed in staring at how perfectly his tailored jacket fit his broad shoulders. Caught, I smiled innocently and waved, praying he couldn't tell I was ogling.

And in that split second, I sensed he might be engaged in the same visual flirtation.

I walked towards the middle of the room, just as he stepped away from the bar. It felt like a giant magnet propelled us towards each other.

Either our strides were perfectly matched, or we had been equidistant from each other all along. Whatever happened, we now stood facing each other in the middle of a vortex of people swirling around us. I felt sure there was no air in the room except for where we stood.

My eyes fixed on his, and his fixed on mine.

He spoke first.

"Well, Kate . . ." he said, not finishing the sentence—and not intending to.

So abrupt did it feel to hear his voice after our prior moment of silent gazing, that I momentarily jumped. Recovering, I giggled and pointed to my arm.

"Oh, my, my." He gasped in mock horror. "Let's dam that up!" Putting his arm around my right shoulder with his hand covering two of the empty grommet holes, he led me to the bar.

And once again, we were facing each other as we had on the train. The swiveling red leather bar stools allowed me to position my good arm fully towards him and my bad arm partially away.

"Bring the lady whatever she wants," he told the bartender. "She's had a bit of a rough day!" I ordered a prosecco and noticed his martini already in place.

"Here's your 'chain of events' tell-all opportunity," he smiled. "I'm dying to know who picked up the other three grommets, and under what circumstances."

An hour later, I had recounted the day's experiences, explaining how I flummoxed the doorman and the building manager with my problem and then underwent a grommet removal procedure by the owner of the dry cleaners, which led to my current look. "Cheap dress," I laughed. "It's a sample size I buy in Texas. At least it's got a story. And now I want to hear yours."

"Time's up!" Christopher answered. "You've got to go, and reluctantly, so do I. But we will do this again. I live in Rye, about an hour north of the City, but I work here. When you get moved in, let's continue. I promise to reveal more about me in good time."

By the time Christopher and I found a way to meet again, a month had passed. In the meantime, I called the owner of the dress store in Texas, who found my missing grommet story hilarious. She pulled strings, sent the dress back to the manufacturer, and got it fully repaired. I also moved into my apartment and was learning to navigate Manhattan.

My second, third, fourth, and fifth meetings with Christopher escalated our attachment. Each time, I was being drawn in more. And each time, I experienced a sense of growing interest on his part.

And every time, I was aware of how fast the evenings ended. There was a reason.

My schedule was somewhat flexible. Christopher's wasn't. Work obligations demanded he get up at 4:30 AM every day to commute into the City. That meant he had to catch a train by 8:30 or 9:00 PM to leave Manhattan and to commute back to Westchester.

So, we worked at seeing each other. Meeting in a romantic bar or restaurant for early dinners, we reluctantly parted so he could make the train home.

The electricity was there on each date. Sparks fueled each conversation. And the kisses went from cautious to less so.

But where was this going?

And then there was an opportunity to find out.

In an unlikely coincidence, Christopher revealed his newly married nephew and bride had just moved blocks from my building in Manhattan.

"I'd like them to meet you. Let me come into the City and take you all to dinner. But there's one problem—they are not available until 8 PM or after. That means I will have to leave following the salad," he teased.

"Ah, but I have the answer to your problem," I said. "Have you ever heard of Chez Somerset? I have a two-bedroom apartment. And as you point out, it's around the corner from your family. Let's have dinner nearby, then stay with me, and you won't have to go home and commute back so early in the morning.

And since you don't know me well, you're welcome to the second bedroom. I promise I won't violate your privacy," I said slyly.

"Oh, but that couldn't work," Christopher said. "I don't have any pajamas."

"You! The former fashion industry executive?! What exactly do you sleep in?" I asked.

"I sleep naked, and I take care not to fry bacon for breakfast."

Trying to lose the visual of his frying bacon in the nude, I asked: "So presuming I can convince you to say yes, what do you like for breakfast?"

"Oh, something healthy . . . like poached eggs, prosciutto, melon, juice, coffee, oatmeal, dry toast. Any and all will be sufficient," he pronounced, jokingly.

With enough coaxing, Christopher agreed to the plan. On the appointed day, he dropped by my building with a small overnight bag he left with Jesse at the front door. Using uncustomary restraint, Jesse said not a word as he tagged it for #18A.

Our dinner reservations were at 8:30 PM at Quality Eats, a nearby restaurant. We were on time, but service was slow. The evening flew by, but the check didn't arrive until 11 PM.

I had never seen Christopher out later than 9 PM. He hung in there, but it was clear he had hit the wall by 10 PM. The last hour of the dinner was an endurance test for him. I was worried he would fall asleep at the table.

Back at the apartment, with his eyes drooping, I could tell Christopher was exhausted.

"Let me get you an extra pillow," I said, directing Christopher to the second bedroom. He didn't protest, and within minutes after he closed the door, I could hear sounds of quiet snoring.

It was midnight. What to do now? I took a shower, put on PJs, went to my bedroom, and stared in the dark at the ceiling. We had enjoyed a wonderful evening, but clearly our body clocks had different rhythms.

Unsure of what was going to happen next, I couldn't go to sleep. Would he wake up in the middle of the night and darken my door? What did I want to have happen? At 4:30 AM, I heard stirring across the apartment. I jumped up and realized he was already in the shower next to the guest room.

Throwing on a robe, I started breakfast. Christopher joined me in the kitchen.

"Good morning! You look beautiful. And check out those peds! Wow, they match the hem of your pajamas," he observed. "Teal and teal!"

What in the world are peds?" I asked.

"Socks," he said. "And you have such great style, you obviously wanted to wear the same color socks as your PJ's . . . not that I can, of course, SEE much of your pajamas under that robe."

"All true," I smiled back. "Those peds didn't much help me get a restful sleep. I admit to being awake most of the night. I am afraid I need a cat nap. What time do you have to leave?" I asked.

"Oh, about 8:00 AM. You go back to bed. I'll bring your pillow back."

Eager to comply, I headed to my bedroom, intending to stay awake for the pillow return. Instead, I was asleep in an instant.

The next thing I knew, I felt a gentle hand on my arm, and lips on mine. I awoke, startled!

"I believe these belong to you," he said, as he tucked something underneath the pillow he had placed back on my bed. Under the pillow were my four grommets. He'd found them in my cabinet in the kitchen while searching for a Keurig cup coffee refill.

I glanced at the clock. It was 7:00 AM.

"Finders keepers!" I said sleepily, and I pulled him towards me.

Closing Reflections

When I decided to write this book, I never stopped thinking about you, the reader. In recounting stories from my dating life, I make myself vulnerable to you. Whether in describing the situations I encountered, how I responded to the men I met, or what decisions I made along the way, I am sharing a slice of my life with you. And my greatest hope is that you will find meaning in my experiences.

The emotions you feel about the subject of dating in mid-life could range from curiosity to amusement to anxiety to surprise. Maybe you are single and have dating stories that rival mine. Maybe you are not yet ready to date but want to know what it's like in the dating world. Maybe you are in a satisfying, committed relationship and happy that you are! Maybe you are the child of newly separated or divorced parents and are trying to understand the dating world they will likely navigate.

If you are single, I would like to think this book will encourage you. If you are unsure about how to approach a man, date online, or carry on a dating conversation, my stories offer you examples. And if you have never been to New York, reading this book will vicariously give you that opportunity. Above all, I hope reading it will help you realize you aren't alone. And I also hope you are entertained.

As I mentioned in the introduction, I never seriously gave thought to dating after my divorce. Even if I could have imagined it, I wouldn't have dreamed I would go out with so many people.

But once I started, I realized how much I enjoyed it. The anticipation, the sense of possibility, the uniqueness of each person, and the chance to develop real friendships intrigued me.

I felt joy, frustration, excitement, disappointment, and awe living the stories you read. More than anything, I marveled at how different each man was—in personality, appearance, life preferences, sense of humor, communication style, level of interest in having a relationship, and in how they reacted to me.

Looking back at the fifteen men as a group illustrates how diverse they are:

- Two never married and have no children.
- Thirteen have children; two have four children each.
- Two introduced me to their children. Four met my daughter.
- Five had been divorced more than ten years. Two were newly divorced in the last year.
- Four are attorneys, one is in medicine, six are entrepreneurs, two have long careers in sales, one is an educator, and another is in civil service.
- Half are six feet or taller. Three are my height.
- One is eleven years older, and one is eleven years younger.
- Five are extroverts. Ten are introverts.
- Three are the life of the party.

- Seven are laid back.
- Five are creative types.
- Eleven are confident. Two have big egos.
- Six are cosmopolitan. Seven like clothes as much as I do.
- Five have big appetites.
- Nine of them care about their cars.
- Eight are well-read. Four have extraordinary vocabularies.
- Six are gifted communicators. Four are captivating public speakers.
- Eight asked great questions.
- Three are naturally very funny.
- Five were fabulous flirts. Four planned inventive, over-the-top dates.
- Three never kissed me. I had chemistry with eight.
- Six understood me.

If I had met fifteen other people, those fifteen stories would have been different.

I am happy to report that a majority of men I have written about would be happy to take a phone call from me. Six are wonderful friends.

One of them wrote me this message:

"I am honored to be included in your book and look forward to reading my chapter with equal parts trepidation, excitement, and imagining! The time I spent with you was some of the most special I have ever had."

Throughout my dating journey, I constantly processed the experiences to understand the takeaways and gain insight.

The three most important lessons dating has taught me are:

1. There is not just one person who is destined for you.

Who we meet and how we fall in love depends on timing, where we live, how much effort and energy we put into making connections, as well as plain old good luck and serendipity. So, take heart. Throughout your life, there are many people you will meet and could have romantic feelings for. My move to New York dramatically changed my options. Not only are there more single people, but they also have more varied interests and backgrounds. That has made dating both an adventure and a challenge. The enormity of the City can make you feel alone and anonymous. I have had to work extra hard at building relationships and staying connected.

2. Dating takes both self-esteem and courage.

Adults who date in mid-life still have the same fears, confidence issues, and self-judging behaviors as teenagers and young adults. We are just older, and time is also shorter. While that doesn't make for less angst, perhaps it makes for less drama! In advance of every date I went on, I felt nervous jitters. To boost my confidence, I turned that adrenaline rush into preparing. That meant I showed up looking my best, gave my complete attention to each man (even if I sensed a second date was not in the offing), asked questions, listened well, and expressed appreciation.

3. Who you will be attracted to—and who is attracted to you—comes down to chemistry.

Impossible to define, chemistry is the sensation of an electric current that passes between two people. There are all kinds of reasons that chemistry is created—attraction to looks, personality, intellect, manners, kindness, generosity, and more. Absent a shared spark, there is often not enough energy or reason to move the connection forward. I usually knew who I found appealing in the first five minutes. It was both a physical and an emotional reaction. I felt a heightened sense of thrill and a stirring of both mind and body.

We all want chemistry. We all want connection. To find it, we must put ourselves in the position to both give and receive.

Anyone can be Kate Somerset. All it takes is the right mindset.

I encourage you to go on your own adventures. Have no preconceived notions. Don't limit yourself. Trust your gut. Use initiative. Don't be afraid. Begin the conversation. You will only find out what awaits you by taking the risk.

May you have the best of fulfilling connections.

In the worst case, you'll have a good story.

In the best case, you may fall in love.

Now, go out and make it happen!

Acknowledgments

To my daughter Ella, who shows me love, laughter, and what it means to believe in second chances.

To the men in this book who have inspired, encouraged, amused, and taught me life is full of delightful surprises.

To my book coach, Aaron Smith, for his direction, reflection, and expert advice over this last year. He lived with the men I wrote about without ever knowing them. And he was able to see story angles I would have missed. For his patience, perspective, and his skillful editing, I am eternally thankful.

To Marina Aris, my publisher and founder of the Brooklyn Writers Press, for taking a chance on this book. I am grateful for her enthusiasm for the message and the meaning.

To Rachel Jellinek of Reflection Films, Inc. for her tireless creative project management skills and introductions to the best illustrator and animator who brought Kate Somerset to life.

To Julia Madden, at Julia Madden Design & Illustration, whose artistic talent and incomparable illustration skills created a compelling and entertaining book cover and chapter introduction pages.

To Jeffrey Long, founder of Mr. Black Media, for his talents in animating Kate to link her to a world of fans.

To Wasabi Publicity for unleashing the magic and the meaning in Kate's stories and message.

To many others who were with me as I wrote this book. I am glad you believed in these stories as much as I love telling them. From New York to Texas and in between, I have felt your love and support.

To all my collaborators, I am inspired by your creativity, good humor, dependability, and talent.

Thank you for making this book and Kate Somerset the real deal.

About the Author

Kate Somerset is a pen name for the author, who three years ago, moved from Texas to New York. A community leader in the nonprofit world, Kate was an established presence in Texas. After her 24-year marriage ended, she decided to pick up stakes and take a chance on a second chapter in Manhattan.

It was a challenging move financially, professionally, and socially. And yet Kate embraced her new life with the sense of what could be. Her dating experiences prove there is always a surprise waiting to happen if you open your mind and heart to the possibilities.

In the several years she's lived in Northeast, Kate has built new relationships, discovered new foods, learned to live in a high-rise building, and braved driving in Manhattan during rush hour. She is delighted that her Texas wardrobe works in the Big Apple (even though she needs a much warmer coat!). Every time she hears that her slightly Southern accent makes her stand out, Kate just smiles.

Although she misses her family, friends, and Texas salsa, Kate delights in life in New York and the opportunity for growing, learning, laughter and love.

THANK YOU FOR READING

Mom, You Just Need to Get Laid
The Adventure of Dating After Divorce

If you enjoyed this book, please consider leaving
a short review on Goodreads or your website of choice.

Reviews help both readers and writers.
They are an easy way to support good work and help to
encourage the continued release of quality content.

Connect with Kate Somerset

www.katesomerset.com

Want the latest from the Brooklyn Writers Press?

Browse our complete catalog www.brooklynwriterspress.com

CPSIA information can be obtained
at www.ICGtesting.com
Printed in the USA
BVHW081914300821
615371BV00003B/8